DISCOVERING
THE JOY OF
OBEDIENCE

By the same author

Discovering How to Pray

When Angels Appear

DISCOVERING THE JOY OF OBEDIENCE

HOPE MacDONALD

Unless otherwise indicated, Scripture references are from The Living Bible, copyright © 1971 by Tyndale House Publishers, Wheaton, Illinois.

Zondervan Publishing House, 1415 Lake Drive, S.E.,
Grand Rapids, Michigan 49506

Library of Congress Cataloging in Publication Data

MacDonald, Hope.
Discovering the joy of obedience.

1. Obedience. I. Title.
BV4647.2M32 248.4 80-29
ISBN 0-310-28521-6

Printed in the United States of America

84 85 86 87 88 — 10 9 8 7 6 5

To my children,
my treasures from God

Thomas Martin MacDonald
Daniel Jay MacDonald
Deborah MacDonald Gronholz

Contents

ACKNOWLEDGMENTS

I want to thank my husband, Harry MacDonald, for his constant encouragement and faithful prayers during the time I wrote this book.

I would never attempt writing a book without a small group of committed, praying friends. These people prayed for me faithfully until the book was finished. The inspiration and help I received from them are much a part of this book.

Sonja Arnold
Shirley Baker
Mildred Burt
Elizabeth Goudge
Jean Griffin
Madalene Harris
Barbara Hanes
Jim Huff
Nancy Kandel
Margaret Logan
Marilyn Mead
Beverly Miller
Judy Penfield
Jane Short

We are no more to think "What should I like to do?" but "What would the Living One have me do?"

George MacDonald
1824–1905

The ROOT of Obedience

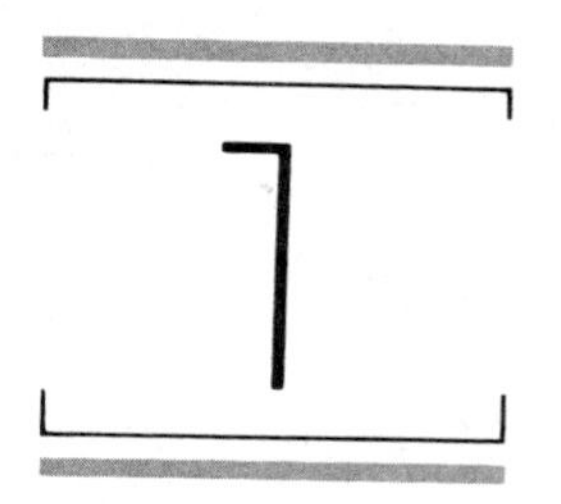

Choosing the Way

Your laws are my joyous treasure forever (Ps. 119:111).

I dreamed I was sitting at the piano playing a duet with someone. The piece was "Chopsticks," and we were playing it as it has been played by children and adults for years. But when we came to the last note, I suddenly added a new chord. It was a beautiful chord and completely unexpected. Those who were listening seemed happy and surprised that something so basic and simple could become so refreshingly lovely.

What made my dream unusual was that I dreamed it the night before I started writing this book on obedience. As I thought about it over breakfast the next morning, I asked, "Lord, do You have a message in this funny little dream for me?"

And these are the thoughts He gave me: Everyone knows obedience is important. It isn't a new truth. But because they have heard it so often, they no longer pay attention to it. You are going to write about the freedom of obedience, and it is going to be a discovery of joy.

God has a happy surprise for all of us, and it comes from the simple, basic chord that runs through the Bible—obedience. It sounds from every page of God's Word, from Genesis to Revelation.

An obedient Christian is one who is committed to God, who lives his or her life under the authority of God's Word, who hears God's Word and does it. I like to compare the Christian life to a train running upon a track. One rail of the track is obedience and the other is dependency. Neither rail can go ahead of the other. They must remain parallel at all times or the train will derail.

Obedience is the guiding principle of the Christian life, and it means total commitment. It means obeying all that Jesus tells us, not just the things we want to obey.

When we begin to live the obedient life, we become open to receiving His love and all He has for us. And then we begin to make the astonishing discovery that we are becoming all God created us to be.

Disobedience is the root of all sin. It is the source of all the evil that fills our world. It is responsible for the heartache and suffering that fill the news on television each day. Above all, disobedience destroys our relationship with God.

Disobedience is rebellion—we want to do it our way. "Have it your way" is the theme of a popular commercial, and it seems to be the philosophy of most people today. We've done away with the God of the Bible. We've made our own little gods of materialism and self-worship, and we are sinking fast into the sea of death called narcissism.

The popular refrain of the modern Christian message has become "All this and heaven too." The bumpers on cars abound with symbols of the cross, the fish, the dove, and catchy slogans of modern theology. Movie stars, politicians, professional athletes, and even pornographers have been pushed, too soon, into the spotlight as Christian celebrities. Christianity has become the greatest show on earth, and in our mad scramble to gather more people under the big top, we have forgotten that Jesus has called us to a life of discipline, commitment, and obedience.

> *The central call of the Gospels, to follow Jesus and become a disciple, is what is most notably absent in the present born-again frenzy.*[1]

Today we have many Christians but little obedience. We have many religious people but few disciples.

OBEDIENCE AS A GOAL

God has a plan for each one of us. He has chosen us for Himself and has set us apart for obedience. His desire is to fill us with His life and His Spirit so we may become new creations in Him (2 Cor. 5:17). God summed this up when He said, "For I know the plans

I have for you, says the Lord. They are plans for good and not for evil, to give you a future and a hope" (Jer. 29:11).

God has a dream for you—a destiny. He dearly loves you, as He claims in His Word, and He wants the best for your life.

What is your dream for your Christian life?

When our daughter, Debbie, was in high school, she was asked to write a paper about her father. She wrote, "My dad dreams dreams and he does them." Are you dreaming any dreams today? And are you *doing* them?

I like the poem written by Bashō, the father of Haiku poetry. When he was eighty-seven years old and on his deathbed, his students gathered around him and asked him to write a poem about dying. He wrote:

On a journey, ill,
and over fields all withered, dreams
go wandering still.[2]

Though Bashō was old, sick, and dying, he had not stopped dreaming.

When Golda Meir returned to the States for a visit, she went to the school she had attended as a child in Milwaukee, Wisconsin. As she addressed the student body that day, she told them that the important decision you make in life is not *what* you'll be; the important decision is to decide upon the *way* you want to live your life.

How different our life would be if we who claim the name of Jesus decided upon the *way* we wanted to live our Christian life—if we had a goal. You've heard the expression, "If you aim at nothing, you'll be sure to hit it." This is exactly what's happening in most of our Christian lives—nothing. We have become a people who are living lukewarm, self-satisfied, self-centered, mediocre Christian lives. We go to church on Sunday with an empty cup and tell the pastor or priest to "fill it up."

How different it would be if we went to church with a full cup. If we would spend the week in the presence of Jesus, whether at work, home, or school, our cup would be full. Then we could leave our place of worship with cups running over because the fullness would have been added to. As a result, during the following week we would be able to touch others with the reality of the love of God.

Before reading any further, take a moment to reflect on your Christian life. Make an active decision about the *way* you want to live it. Don't expect it to "just happen" because it won't. You need a goal, a dream, something for which to strive. You need to aim to become a vital, obedient Christian.

I believe there is a great longing on the part of all believers to be close to Jesus, to regain that first love we had when we came to Him as Savior. But the question is, how much are we willing to do to be close to Him? A little discipline—a little commitment—a little obedience? We must be willing to be "obedient unto death," as Philippians says. Would you be willing to die for Jesus?

In this book I will not be setting down a list of

rules for living the obedient life. There aren't any rules. Each person lives his or her own life with God; He is always the God of the individual. But I will be sharing some basic principles about the joyful, abundant, obedient life God wants for His children.

There won't be any simple lists of dos and don'ts. We've all had plenty of those down through the years, and they have accomplished nothing but division. Christians have spent centuries throwing stones at each other in the name of Jesus. And at what a price!

Listen to some of the man-made rules Christians tried to force upon other Christians in the second century:

> *Colored clothes, for one thing. Get rid of everything in your wardrobe that is not white. Stop sleeping on a soft pillow. Sell your musical instruments and don't eat any more white bread. You cannot, if you are sincere about obeying Christ, take a warm bath or shave your beard. To shave is to lie against Him who created us, to attempt to improve on His word.*[3]

We may smile and shake our head as we read that, but we are much like the Christians of the second century. We still have our strange little man-made molds into which we try to pour others. We still insist that unless they obey our rules we will not accept them.

My purpose in writing this book is to direct us back to the basic principle of the Word of God—obedience. To focus our attention upon Jesus. To find out where we got off the track and how we can get back on.

May your goal and your dream be to become Christlike in your love—your love for God and your love for others—and to become Christlike in your obedience. God's great call is still the same as it was 2000 years ago: "Come and see." Come and see what will happen as you make obedience to Him your life goal. Come and see what it means to be free as you experience the joy of obedience.

A Glimpse of Splendor

The Lord is good and glad to teach the proper path to all who go astray; he will teach the ways that are right and best to those who humbly turn to him. And when we obey him, every path he guides us on is fragrant with his loving-kindness and his truth (Ps. 25:8–10).

A few months ago my daughter, Debbie, had an extraordinary dream. She dreamed she and her husband, Marc, were driving down a busy street. It was rush hour, and the traffic was bumper to bumper. Suddenly, above the din on the highway she heard the faint sound of trumpets. Looking up, she saw a brilliant light break through the darkening clouds of evening. The sky burst into color as if heaven had opened its door just a crack and pushed out some of its splendor. A group of angels gathered, blowing the trumpets of heaven. And in the midst of all this, Jesus appeared—coming in the clouds of glory just as He said He would. In an instant Debbie was out of the car, onto the sidewalk, and down on her knees.

When she awoke, she was actually kneeling in her bed. As she related this dream to me, her brown eyes filled with tears of wonder. She said it was one of the most powerful experiences of her life because she had realized for the first time that all that matters in life is Jesus. "Nothing—nothing—not even Marc—can compare to the great wonder and glory of seeing Jesus."

Who is this Jesus who by His very presence causes us to fall on our knees in worship and adoration? Who is this One about whom Scripture says: "At the name of Jesus every knee shall bow in heaven and on earth and under the earth, and every tongue shall confess that Jesus Christ is Lord, to the glory of God the Father" (Phil. 2:10–11)? Before we can obey Him, we need to understand something of who He is and what He has done. We need to glimpse His splendor.

First, He is the majestic God of the universe who revealed Himself to us through His marvelous creation. He is the God of power and strength. All of nature obeys His simple word of command. He is the God who is in complete control of all things.

Our planet Earth is part of the solar system. At

the heart of our solar system is the sun which is a star. The nearest star to our planet, other than the sun, is a star called Alpha Centauri which is four and a half light-years away. A light-year is about 5,880,000,000,000 miles. To give an idea of how far that is: If you boarded an Apollo spacecraft and left the earth in A.D. 1 and traveled nonstop until A.D. 2000, you would be less than one tenth of 1 percent of the way to Alpha Centauri, our nearest star.

Then think about this. Our planet Earth is in a galaxy called the Milky Way. On a clear night you can look up into the sky and see a part of this galaxy stretched across the heavens. Scientists tell us there are over 200,000,000,000 stars in the Milky Way. And there are another billion galaxies just like it in the universe![1]

Considering these facts is like parting the curtain just a sliver and getting a glimpse into the vast mysteries of the universe. Yet even this glimpse taxes our imagination beyond its limits of comprehension.

Listen to what one powerful passage in the Bible says about the One who created all this: "Now Christ is the visible expression of the invisible God. He existed before creation began, for it was through him that everything was made, whether spiritual or material, seen or unseen. . . . In fact, every single thing was created through, and for, him. He is both the first principle and the upholding principle of the whole scheme of creation" (Col. 1:15–17 PHILLIPS).

If you want to understand something about God, take a look at the universe. There you will begin to discover His greatness. Take a look at nature, and you will begin to learn about His creativity. Take a look at the Bible, and you will see what He has to say about Himself and about life and how to live it.

But there is another aspect of who God is that dwarfs the above information: "The Word became flesh and lived for a while among us" (John 1:14 NIV). All the mystery of life, for time and eternity, is summed up in that one mighty statement. "At the beginning God expressed himself. That personal expression, that word, was with God, and was God, and he existed with God from the beginning. All creation took place through him, and none took place without him.... So the word of God became a human being and lived among us. We saw his splendour ... full of grace and truth" (John 1:1–4, 14 PHILLIPS).

This sovereign Creator-God-Redeemer scaled Himself down to our size and lived among us. He entered into human history, and this infinitesimal planet Earth became His home for thirty-three years. What a Visitor from another world—the almighty, triune God of the universe!

This is the living One who demands and deserves our obedience.

3 Where It Begins

Those who love your laws have great peace of heart and mind and do not stumble (Ps. 119:165).

I was sitting at a picnic table with four new friends in Vancouver, British Columbia. It was a warm spring day, and the flowers had just begun to bloom. The air was heavy with their fragrance. Our table was under a big shade tree in a rather secluded section of the park. As we finished our lunch, we began sharing with each other how we had met Jesus as Savior.

Peggy was sitting across the table from me, and I could tell she could hardly wait until it was her turn to share. She told us briefly about her life as a wealthy society woman in New England. She had had a beautiful home, lovely children, and a husband who loved her. Yet she had known something was missing from her life.

Then one spring Billy Graham had come to the area for a series of meetings. Of course she had heard about this famous "Bible-preaching evangelist," and she thought it might be amusing to go and hear what he had to say.

When she arrived at the meeting, she was amazed at the thousands of people who were there. What could they possibly be doing at a place like this?

As she was ushered to a seat, she looked around her a bit self-consciously, hoping she wouldn't see anyone she knew. What would they think of her? None of her friends would understand. She didn't hear any of the sermon because she was too busy looking around at all the people, noticing what they were wearing and wondering why they had come.

At the end of the message, Graham gave an invitation for anyone who would like to receive Jesus as Savior to come forward. Peggy came to attention at this and watched in astonishment as hundreds of people stood to their feet and began moving forward. And as she was watching, she saw a picture of Jesus standing under a tree with a group of people sitting around Him on the ground. Then he looked at Peggy with a smile on His face and asked her, "Would you like to come and sit here with Me?"

It was as simple as that. Peggy realized she had a choice to make. So she stood to her feet and went forward—toward Jesus. (Here her face broke into a radiant smile.) As she took her first step toward Him, she said she was *instantly* filled with a spirit of peace and love such as she had never experienced in all her life.

Peggy had made that decision several years ago, and she told us what Christ had come to mean to her and to her entire family. She had said a simple yes to Jesus, and her life was completely changed. She discovered she had a new relationship with the God of the universe, she had a new relationship with others, and she had a new relationship with herself.

Her first act of obedience to God came when she heard Him say to her, "Would you like to come and sit here with Me?" and she chose, by an act of her will, to walk toward Him. Such a simple thing, and yet her life was never the same after that moment.

Our first act of obedience to God comes the moment we hear Him say to us, "Come and follow Me." When we hear His voice and take that first step toward Him, then all of life begins anew.

WHAT IS A CHRISTIAN?

Because of my husband's job as International Coordinator of Young Life, we have the unique privilege of traveling to many parts of the world. When we travel to another country, we are always struck by this one thing: America is still looked upon as a Christian nation.

This fact came through clearly during a visit to India. While there, we were invited to the home of an Indian family. We looked forward to being in an Indian home and getting to know what family life was like. We had spent several days walking the crowded, death-filled streets and were beginning to wonder if there was such a thing as home and family life in that country. Our hearts had been broken to the point of despair at the tragedy of India. It was a welcome change to enter the cool courtyard, walk up on the veranda, and be ushered into the quietness of a living room.

They had invited their entire family to meet the Americans. All the children, aunts, uncles, and grandparents were there to greet us with open curiosity. We were the first Americans they had ever had in their home.

After dinner we sat around the table visiting, and at one point my husband, Harry, reached into his pocket and pulled out some American coins to give to the children. After looking at them carefully, one of the older boys asked him what was printed on them. When Harry said, "In God we trust," the entire room became quiet. Then everyone wanted to see the money—the men, the women, and all the children. They held them reverently, and with awe they asked, "Do you mean *all* of your coins say, 'In God we trust'?" They thought America must be a great nation to have such a thing printed on its money.

I tell this little story to point up the fact that we do live in an unusual country. Other nations of the world still look to America as a Christian nation. Even though we are living in a post-Christian era, we are reaping the rewards of our Christian heritage. However, many people have the idea that just because they are born in America they are automatically Christian, and this is not so. No one is born a Christian.

Do you know what a Christian is? Could you explain it simply to someone at work or at school? Do you know how to tell your children what a Christian is, or are you leaving that up to the church? God holds us, as believers, responsible for teaching others what it means to be Christ's one.

There are many things that make up the Christian life, but basically a Christian is "one in whom God dwells." Now the only way He can dwell within you is if you choose, by an act of your will, to ask Him to come into your life, as Peggy did when she heard Him ask her to come and sit under the tree with Him.

To become a Christian is to repent. Some people don't like that word, but it simply means "to want to be different." You realize you are on the wrong road, and you want to get on the right one. Repentance means getting off the wrong road in life and getting on the right one with Jesus. It means turning away *from* sin and turning *towards* God.

To become a Christian means to be forgiven. Forgiven from what? From your sin. There is no way you can understand your need to repent unless you know you are a sinner who desperately needs a Savior. The Bible tells us, "All have sinned; all fall short of God's glorious ideal" (Rom. 3:23). And the Bible also tells us Jesus died on the cross to save sinners.

You need to see Jesus dying on the cross for your sin. You must see yourself at the cross, picking up the hammer and pounding the nails into His hands. I remember the first time I saw myself doing that—I turned away in horror and said, "No, Lord, I would never do that." And He said, "Unless you see yourself pounding the nails into My hands, you will never fully understand that it was for *you* I died."

Christ didn't die on the cross to show you by example that He is love. He didn't hang there so you could go to heaven. He hung there for one reason and one reason only—to die for your sin. You need to understand that you are a sinner in desperate need of a Savior.

Forgiveness is one of the most beautiful words in any language. To be forgiven means "to have the record wiped clean." It means to live in the joy of being completely forgiven, not just once, but endlessly, every day. To be a Christian means to be cleansed and welcomed into the family of God. The Bible tells us that the angels sing a hymn of praise over every person who receives Jesus as Savior.

Have the angels ever sung over you?

Obedience to Jesus Christ must start at the foot of the cross.

The Luminous Glow and the Dark Dogma

God's laws are perfect. They protect us, make us wise, and give us joy and light. God's laws are pure, eternal, just. They are more desirable than gold. They are sweeter than honey dripping from a honey-comb. For they warn us away from harm and give success to those who obey them (Ps. 19:7–11).

It was the Fourth of July, and we were sitting in the Los Angeles coliseum. We had just watched a spectacular display of fireworks. The bands had marched, the patriotic anthems had been sung, and the last wisp of smoke from the fireworks was drifting off towards the Pacific Ocean. Suddenly the lights of the coliseum went out, leaving us in total darkness. A voice from the loudspeaker said, "Ladies and gentlemen, if you will each take the match you were given when you came in and light it, you will see something that will outshine everything else seen here tonight." And then, one by one, flickering lights began to appear, until finally each person held a lighted match and the coliseum was bathed in a brilliant, glowing splendor.

I have never forgotten that sight, although it happened many years ago. I can still feel the excitement that swept through that stadium as the light from 100,000 matches broke through the darkness. It was a moment of glory.

Jesus said we are to be the light of the world; we are to shine out brightly in the darkness. Then those around us will see our radiant lives and "glorify . . . (our) Father which is in heaven" (Matt. 5:16 KJV).

When Dr. Christiaan Barnard performed the first heart transplant, he needed a patient who was willing to be obedient and put his life into the doctor's hands. After the operation had proven successful, it was Dr. Barnard who received the honor and glory. His picture was splashed on the front page of newspapers around the world. Few people remembered the name of the patient who had the operation. Yet it was through his life that Dr. Barnard received the honor and glory due him.

What does it mean to glorify God or be a glory to God? The pages of the Bible ring with this phrase:

"You will see more of his glory" (Exod. 16:7).

"The glory of the Lord rested upon Mt. Sinai" (Exod. 24:16).

"The Tabernacle shall be sanctified by my glory" (Exod. 29:43).

"The landscape shone bright with the glory of the Lord" (Luke 2:9).

What does it mean when someone says, "The glory of the Lord touches every person she ministers to." Or, "When he walks into the dark hovels of death, the glory of the Lord suddenly fills the room." Or, "her face shines with the glory of the Lord."

The Glory of God always seemed such a nebulous phrase to me, something I couldn't grasp. Then one day I found a definition I could understand. William Barclay, in his commentary on John, says, "The glory of God is the luminous glow of the Presence of God." Isn't that great? It has given me a completely new perspective on what the glory of God means.

This glow of the presence of God may actually be seen in our lives. The luminous glow of His presence can fill our homes. It can touch our relationships with our mates. Our children can see this luminous glow and, as a result, want to know Jesus. People can warm their hands and their hearts at the luminous glow they see in our lives.

Talk about life having meaning and purpose? Think what it would mean if all who claim the name of Jesus were to be filled with the luminous glow of His presence. Our world would be different, our homes would be different, our relationships with one another would be different, and the Father in heaven would receive the honor He deserves.

We would be like the lights that filled the coliseum that night. Our lives would be bathed in the glowing splendor of the presence of God, and people everywhere would know that the Light of the World is Jesus.

This truth must become the driving force to motivate us to live the obedient Christian life. We must want to be obedient to God for no other reason than that our life will bring glory to Him. This must become our goal, our dream—that our lives will be filled with the luminous glow of the presence of God.

One of the most influential Christian creeds says, "The chief end of humanity is to glorify God and enjoy Him forever."

THE DARK DOGMA

Unfortunately, another philosophy is subtly taking its place in our lives. This philosophy says, "The chief end of man is his own happiness." This philosophy, called humanism, says whatever makes a person happy is all right. Personal happiness becomes the goal of life. Or to put it in a modern cliché, "If it feels good, do it." Never mind if it will hurt others: that's their problem. Never mind if it breaks up a family and destroys children. Happiness is all that matters. As a result, each person becomes an island, isolated in a desperate search for happiness. Any current magazine or newspaper shows the devastating results this humanistic philosophy has produced.

But the real tragedy is that humanism has insidiously crept into the lives of Christians.

I was speaking at a women's retreat in the northwest recently. One afternoon I took a quiet walk to Puget Sound. The tide was out, and I climbed up on a moss-covered rock to be alone with God. The sound of crunching seashells soon interrupted my thoughts, and I turned to see an attractive young woman walking toward me. She was one of the women from the retreat, and I invited her to sit with me. After a few moments of remarking about the beauty that surrounded us, we began talking about prayer.

She said, "You know, Hope, I used to pray a lot. But I stopped recently because it seemed God never answered my prayers."

She had the erroneous idea that prayer is just asking God for things. If we don't get what we ask for, we say, "I guess prayer doesn't work." It's almost as though we make God our errand boy. We give Him our list of things we want Him to do for us that day, and if they don't get finished on time or the way we want them, we fire Him. Unconsciously, our attitude towards prayer becomes very humanistic: What am I going to get out of it? If God doesn't answer my prayers, then why should I pray?

Prayer is much more than just asking God for things. It's sharing our lives with the God of the universe. It's having fellowship with the One who loves us and gave Himself for us. It's walking with Jesus. It's talking with Him. Prayer is being *with Jesus.*

The contemporary questions, "How will this benefit me?" "How much can I get out of this?" "What's in it for me?" have dominated even our presentation of the gospel. Many new converts are never taught what it means to be a Christian. If they can nod their heads to a few spiritual questions, they are welcomed into the family of God. People respond to the gospel so they can have peace, joy, and go to heaven. Everything is done for their personal happiness. "God is in heaven for our happiness, all the angels exist for our happiness and Jesus died on the cross for our happiness."[1]

They want happiness and comfort, and if Christ can do this—great—they'll add Him to their lives (sort of like adding a cherry on top of a hot fudge sundae). Jesus adds that extra touch to life.

The newly converted editor of a pornographic magazine summed up our humanistic Christianity well when he said that in the future his magazine would carry "sex and Christ." The thought that Jesus makes a difference in our moral behavior is rarely included in a call to come to Jesus. A head deacon, who was living in an adulterous situation, recently stamped out of the pastor's study in a rage when he was told he could no longer be a deacon. "You're nothing but a narrow-minded bigot," he screamed at the pastor as he slammed the door. A man in the South is attracting thousands of businessmen to his meetings. His great drawing card is "Religion without the negative aspects." He promises his listeners riches on earth and no moral standards. He focuses not on what we can do for God, but on what God wants to do and can do for us *right now.*

We need to be reminded again that "The characteristics of the gospel that are least marketable—self-sacrifice, servanthood, the way of the cross, identification with the poor and oppressed, a prophetic voice to the state, a life of simplicity and sharing, justice and peace—are those characteristics that don't get communicated to the society."[2]

The gospel message has been watered down so much that what we have left is simply a good way for man to achieve his humanistic goals regardless of what they may be. We have so sugar-coated God's truth that it has become all sugar and very little truth.

We are living in a totally self-centered, humanistic culture. Self-fulfillment and self-satisfaction have become our gods and have replaced the God of the Bible. "The question today is 'What can Jesus do for me? How can He make me happier, more content, more successful, better adjusted and more prosperous?'"[3] God is presented as a miniature Santa Claus who gives us everything we want. His sole purpose of existence is to meet our needs. All we have to do is whistle and God will come running, ready to grant our every desire. "The chief end of man is his own happiness" has become our religion, infiltrating our Christian living so subtly that it has caught us totally unaware.

We must return to the creed our faith is built

upon, "The chief end of humanity is to glorify God." The purpose of living the obedient life is to give God the glory He deserves. If we have any other reason for living the obedient life, we will fail.

The REALITY of Obedience

5 The Three Loves

I would have you learn this great fact: that a life of doing right is the wisest life there is (Prov. 4:11).

In the Christian life there are three significant love relationships that must be recognized: God's love for us; our love for God; and our love for one another. It is so easy to become complacent in the joy of God's love for us that we forget about the necessity of loving one another. And sometimes we become so totally absorbed in our warm, cozy love for Jesus that we forget the tremendous implication of His great love for us. These three love relationships must be operative in our lives if we are going to live the kind of meaningful, joy-filled, obedient life God has waiting for us.

Do you have difficulty believing God loves you? That He loves you just as you are, this moment, with all your imperfections? I had this problem for years. I never doubted that God loved the world. Hadn't I memorized John 3:16? "For God so loved the world, that he gave his only begotten Son, that whosoever believeth in him should not perish, but have everlasting life" (KJV). I knew God loved the world. I knew He loved my children. I knew He loved my husband. And I knew He loved all my neighbors. But *me?* I knew He loved the prisoners and the derelicts. I knew He loved the millionaires and the jet-setters. I knew He loved the Russians and the Chinese and everyone else around the world. But somehow I could never grasp the fact that God loved me.

It wasn't that I thought I was unlovable. I knew my parents had always loved me; I knew my friends cared for me; I knew my husband dearly loved me; and I knew my children loved me. But I couldn't grasp the truth that God loved me.

Then a few years ago when we were serving as missionaries in Brazil, God made His love known to me. (I also never doubted for a single moment that God loved the Brazilians!) I was sitting in bed reading one night. It was winter in Brazil, and our house with its thick stone walls was cold and damp. Because we didn't have central heat, the only warm place was in bed under the electric blanket we had brought with us from the States. In the quietness of that cold Brazilian bedroom, God spoke to me. He said, "Hope, do you love Me?" And I replied, "Lord, You *know* I love You." This was another fact I had never doubted since I had given my life to Jesus when I was ten years old. I knew I loved God. When I told Him this, He said to me, "Don't you know you are able to love Me only because *I first loved you.*" Wow! It was like a blinding light! I saw for the first time the ancient truth, "We love him, because he first loved us" (1 John 4:19 KJV). How had I overlooked it? I had memorized that verse before I started school! As the reality of His love *for me* engulfed me for the first time, I wanted to get out of bed and jump for joy. I wanted to climb to the top of the roof and shout to the world, "Wake up! God loves me!" It was a moment I will never forget. Since then I have never doubted His love for me.

Do you know that God loves you right now? *You.* I'm not talking about your friend or your husband. I'm talking about you.

If we want to live an obedient Christian life, we must understand that the great God of the universe loves us because His love for us is the foundation of our life. Obedience stems from God's love being perfected in us. A poster I saw recently said, "Love is something you do." Obedience to God is our love in action. It is a demonstration of our love for Him in response to His great love for us.

I was visiting our son Tom in Nevada City, California. We were having Sunday brunch together in the picturesque dining room of an old museum. I enjoy talking with Tom because he has many interesting insights into what is happening in our culture today. He went through the drug scene a few years back, and it is encouraging to see how God is gently making Himself known in Tom's life again.

Over our gourmet breakfast of shirred eggs and pastries, we began talking about God. Tom said, "At times it's very difficult for me to comprehend all the things I've heard about God. I can't seem to put it all together." I could identify with him because I had often felt the same way.

I said, "Tom, for now forget everything you've heard about God. Forget all the thoughts and ideas you've been mulling over in your mind these past few years and zero in on this one thing: 'God so loved the world that he gave.' Put a period after it right there. Think about that one sentence. Meditate on it when you're alone because everything you need to know about God is summed up in that one sentence.

"In it you discover two things. First, you see He is a loving God. He loves the whole world. Not just America. Not just the 'good' people. Not just the people who love Him. He loves the world. He loves the person who loves Him, and He loves the one who never gives Him a second thought. He loves the one who receives His love and the one who rejects it. Everyone is included in the little phrase, 'God so loved the world.' He loves you, and He loves every person here in Nevada City."

I could sense Tom grappling with this truth as we continued eating our breakfast. After a few moments of silence, I said, "The thing that sets Christianity apart from every other world religion can be summed up in the last two words, 'he gave.' God always takes the first step toward us. He is the One who reaches His hand out to us first. Try to grasp what that means. Someday you will be able to take the rest of John 3:16 and apply it to your life, but start with this first phrase, Tom. Because as long as you live, you will never hear a greater truth summed up in one sentence—'God so loved the world that he gave.'"

Tom put down his fork slowly and, with a look of thoughtful surprise, said in all sincerity, "That's dynamite, mom."

And you know something? He was right.

Have you discovered the dynamite of God's individual love for you? Saint Augustine said, "God loves each one of us as if there was only one of us to love." Everything in our Christian life springs from this truth, "God so loved the world that he gave." It is the starting point for obedient living.

OUR LOVE FOR GOD

Love is the silken chord that binds us to Christ

When we choose, by an act of our will, to live the obedient life, we must answer one question. *Do I really love God?* Do I love Him more than anything in all the world? Do I love Him more than my family? More than my friends? More than my career? More than the comforts that surround me? Can we say as Peter did, "You know that I love You, Lord." And in the knowing, we must understand that our love for Him is simply the reflection of His love for us.

When we can say this in confidence, God's love will grip our life in such a way that we will not need to be told what we should or should not do. I hate that, don't you? Always being told? My husband's father used to say to him, "Go and tell your mother you love her." This created a sense of rebellion in Harry's heart. He loved his mother, and he would tell her so from time to time, but he hated to be told to tell her. Likewise, when we are forced to adhere to man-made religious rules, we often rebel.

As we learn to love Jesus more and long to follow Him on the obedient pathway, we see for ourself the right way to go and we know from within the right thing to do. Thus, the foundation of our obedient life is built upon the reality of God's love for us and our love for Him.

OUR LOVE FOR OTHERS

There are two foundation stones (principles) in the Christian life:

1. our love for Jesus
2. our love for others

We learn the first one, and we practice the second. If we think we hear God telling us to do something that is not in harmony with these two principles, we have not heard correctly.

When we lose our love for one another, we lose

everything of value in this life. We become critical, judgmental people. Harry and I saw this happen in Brazil. We went there to start the work of Young Life. None of the students we worked with were Christians. They would come to our home each Sunday afternoon because that was the only day they didn't have school or work. Many of them traveled two hours in order to get there. Often we would have over a hundred young people crowded into our house and garden. They would play games and talk. Small groups filled every corner of the house. After an afternoon of fellowship, we would have our meeting in the early evening.

Because many of these students did not have record players at home, some would bring their latest jazz records over and use our phonograph. Unfortunately, in her "rule book of Christian living," one of the other missionaries in our area had the law that no jazz should be played in a Christian home. This person felt God was telling her to alert other young people not to come to our home. Soon rumors had to be tacked onto her rules to emphasize them, and these rumors were passed throughout the missionary community. One absurd rumor was that we locked our three children in their bedrooms when the students came because we didn't want the Brazilians to know we were old enough to have teen-agers! Although we did not go to Brazil to minister to missionaries, we missed the desperately needed fellowship that could have been ours if we had not broken some man-made "rules of Christianity."

Because of this experience, years later I could identify with my new Christian friend who called me on the telephone and said with tears of frustration, "I'm sick of being around Christians. All they do is hurt me, criticize me, pull me apart, and leave me in small broken pieces."

Is this how you feel about some of God's people? Is this how people feel about you?

Many Christians have forgotten the basic principle of loving one another. We have lost our first love, our love for Jesus, and consequently our love for others has grown cold. People can no longer warm their hearts at the fire of our love because even the dying embers have turned to ashes.

The only way we're going to succeed in our life of obedience is to begin again to love God and to love others as we love ourself. We can be good missionaries, good social workers, good Bible teachers, good students, and good people, but if we lose our love for one another, we have lost the essence of Christian living.

What does the Bible mean when it says we are to love our neighbor as ourself? In today's transient society, do we even know who our neighbor is? George MacDonald said, "My neighbor is the one who is next to me at that moment."

When Jesus gave us this commandment, He was telling us we are to love our neighbor in the same way that we already love and care for ourself. He was not promoting the "self-love" philosophy that is springing up all over our nation today.

Jesus is not calling for self-love. He assumes that it already exists. As far as we know, Jesus never entertained the thought that there could be someone who didn't love himself. To use the words of Paul in Ephesians 5:29, "No man ever hates his own flesh but nourishes and cherishes it."[1]

We may need to improve our self-esteem or our self-image (most of us need help in this area), but not our self-love. Unless we are emotionally ill, we already care for ourself. We make sure we have enough food to eat, although there are millions who do not. We insist people treat us right, and we are offended when snubbed and hurt when neglected. We want the "best seat in the house" when we go to a symphony or a play. When I called to make reservations for a play recently, I told the operator the price range we could afford and then said, "We want the best seats as close to the middle and near the front as we can get." I didn't say, "Give us the worst seats please, the ones behind the pillar, so others who call in later can have the better ones" It didn't even occur to me to say that. I wanted the best. I see this principle of self-love lived out in my life every day, just as Jesus assumed it would be.

If someone criticizes us, we defend ourself and set the record straight, as I saw clearly in a friend who had returned from a marriage encounter weekend. She was bubbling over as she shared the helpful insights she had learned. Suddenly she reached into her purse and pulled out a crumpled sheet of paper. One of the workshop assignments had been to make a list of things that irritated them about their spouses. Then they were to sit down together and go over the lists and try to find some solution. "Now just listen to this," she said defiantly—and down the list she went, reading every item her husband had put down. After each one she stopped, took off her glasses, and offered an excuse or reason why she did that thing. As she stuffed the paper back into her purse, she said indignantly, "He didn't have to make such a long list!"

The thing that interested me was the way she excused herself in *every* situation. As I was driving home, I thought, This must be the way we are supposed to love others. This must be what Jesus meant when He told us to love our neighbor as we already love ourself. We are to excuse their faults. We are to love and excuse them in spite of their strange little flaws, just as we love and excuse ourself.

Does it seem impossible that you could love others this way? Will you dare to try it? Once we catch a glimpse of the liberty and happiness that come into our lives when we no longer live for self alone, we will wonder why we hung on so desperately to the "I."

Jesus is calling us to a life of learning what it means to be a loving person. He asks that we be filled with compassion and mercy and gentleness.

This is part of the adventure of obedient Christian living.

6 Our High Calling

He has told you what he wants, and this is all it is: to be fair and just and merciful, and to walk humbly with your God (Micah 6:8).

The holidays were over. The tree had been taken down, and the last Christmas decoration had been packed away for another year. The "day of reckoning" had arrived. I stepped on the scales and noted the sad truth I had suspected—fifteen pounds overweight! How could little butter cookies and cranberry nut bread turn into such unsightly fat? As I walked into the kitchen, a cloud of gloom hovered over me. "Look how fat I've gotten during the holidays," I told my husband. I was certain he would reassure me by saying he loved every little extra pound of me, but he didn't. Instead he said, "Looks like you'll have to go on a diet."

Well, I started my diet three weeks ago and have lost five pounds. I am picturing myself thin and elegant, wearing my favorite dress that hasn't fit all winter. Picturing myself thin helps me achieve my goal.

All that we do begins with a mind picture. I have found this to be a basic truth about life. Every great and horrible deed is first conceived in the mind. Before an artist begins a painting, he sees in his mind the finished canvas. Authors, inventors, murderers, thieves, all see in their mind a plan of what they want to accomplish. When the picture becomes clear, it is put into action.

When we constantly tell our children, "You're so bad," or "You never do anything right," we can count on their being bad and not doing anything right. On the other hand, when we tell them how good they are or how proud we are of them, this picture of goodness is planted in the mind and becomes a goal.

This is how it is with the obedient life. We see in our mind the new person God created us to be and we strive for that picture—that goal. When we choose, by an act of our will, to become an obedient Christian, then all of life becomes governed by the principle stated so well by George MacDonald, the famous English author: "We are no more to think what should I like to do, but what would the Living One have me do?"

A few years ago I began trying to live by this. Our

daughter had just gotten married. She was the last of the children to leave home, and it was a period of real adjustment for me. Shortly after the wedding, Harry had to go to Europe on business for three weeks. I found myself alone in the house for the first time in my life. I managed to get by fairly well the first week, but by the middle of the second week I felt utterly lost and alone. The house seemed so quiet. I thought I would even welcome the sound of Debbie's loud records mingled with the incessant ringing of the telephone. (You know you're desperate when you reach that point!)

As I sat in the quiet living room, a cloud of depression began to settle over me and a case of self-pity set in. I began to cry. "How could Harry leave me so soon after Debbie's wedding?" I asked the empty room. And the more I cried the deeper I sank into the sea of despair.

Now there's nothing wrong with crying. "But," said one wise person, "don't cry longer than fifteen minutes. Anything longer than a fifteen-minute cry leads to depression. But a short cry is like a shower—it washes away all the strain and tension." At that point I had gone way beyond my allotted fifteen minutes and was sinking fast. In fact, I was thinking of crying all night so that when Harry came home I could tell him I had "spent the entire night in tears." That should sound dramatic!

At that point the Lord entered the scene and said, "Hope, what's that principle you've been trying to live by recently?"

I stopped crying long enough to say, "You mean, what is Your will for me in the midst of this situation?"

And He said, "That's the one."

I must say, I was a bit miffed that He should bring this up when He could plainly see how miserable I was! That wasn't at all what I had in mind when I so nobly told Him I wanted to live by that principle. With a martyred sigh I asked, "All right, Lord, what is Your will for me right now in the midst of this situation?"

All was silent for a moment. Then He said, "I want you to go and play the piano."

"He's got to be kidding!" I thought. The last thing in the world I wanted to do was play the piano. But because I am committed to being obedient, I dragged myself over to the piano and with great sobs of self-pity began to play my favorite classical music. Then I got out my hymnal and began to play and sing. At 11:30 that night I was still at the piano, singing at the top of my voice. I didn't even want to go to bed!

What a great adventure God has waiting for us in the obedient life. He can take a depressing, lonely evening and turn it into something uplifting and affirming. Life can't be too dull with this kind of obedient living!

My husband and I don't argue much, but a few nights ago we were having a real disagreement. Now that's all right because no two people can live together for any length of time and agree on everything. Thirty years of "yes dear" would be pretty monotonous. It's been said, "If you never have an argument, one of you isn't necessary!" Well. Harry and I are both necessary. However, this particular argument was getting out of hand. We had begun to drag old things up from the past that had nothing to do with the problem. In the midst of it all, the Lord came to me with *that* question again. As I waited for Harry to finish drawing his line of battle, I said to God, "Well, what is Your will for me now in the midst of this situation?" The answer came back, "I want you to shut up!" Startled at such a reply, I said, "I will, Lord, but first let me make two more important points." And He said, "No. *Now!*" And I shut up. Once again I saw what God can do with our obedience. I watched Him turn a hostile evening into something pleasant.

Obedience to Him always brings out the best in us.

NO RULE BOOKS

God wants His people to have a spirit of obedience. He wants disciples who are willing to say with the psalmist, "Just tell me what to do and I will do it, Lord" (Ps. 119:33–34). This kind of obedience stems from a new heart, not from a book of rules. "And I will give you a new heart—I will give you new and right desires—and put a new spirit within you. I will take out your stony hearts of sin and give you new hearts of love." (Ezek. 36:26).

Living the obedient life is learning how to live life as God intended it to be. It's learning how to become the people God created us to be. "True holiness consists in doing God's will with a smile."[1]

The Bible was never meant to be a rule book. Rather, it tells us what God is like and how He wants us to live. However, it does spell out specific areas where we are to obey. For example, the Epistles tell us we are to put from our lives all immorality, impurity, evil desire, anger, malice, slander, foul talk, and lying (Col. 3:5–11; Gal. 5:19–25). When we face these things in our life, there isn't any question about what God expects of us. The Ten Commandments were given to show us God's standard of perfection and how far short we fall. But much of our obedient living is not so simply, though profoundly, laid down in black and white. We are not puppets on a string; God expects us to think. He expects us to listen to the leading of the Holy Spirit. He expects us to learn to use our mental and spiritual capacities.

Sometimes we may think it would be easier to live with a set of rules so we would know exactly what was expected of us. There is a certain degree of security in having everything spelled out with no decisions required. This happened to the children of Israel. As long as they were slaves of the Egyptians, they had taskmasters who told them exactly what they must do. They could scarcely take a breath without permission. But when God set them free and Moses led them into the Promised Land, they suddenly became uncertain and insecure. They discovered they faced daily choices, and this was often very threatening. Freedom was not "free."

People are much the same today. The three hundred new cults that have sprung up in our country in recent years are partially a result of people looking for a leader who will lay down specific laws which must be followed. Those looking for this kind of life breathe a sigh of relief when they find a group where everything is decided for them and where they don't have any personal confrontation with the living God but look instead to a human leader. Jonestown is a good example of this.

When we begin to live the obedient life, we often have the mistaken idea that God suddenly is going to tell us every move to make. We find ourself frantically listening for His directions in all we do. We wait for Him to say, "Brush your teeth *now* and use only Crest toothpaste!" Or we're sure He said, "Put exactly fifty-seven cents in the missionary envelope at church." And, "Wear your black shoes instead of your brown ones." In our desire to be obedient, we forget He has given us a mind and expects us to use it. He has given us freedom of choice and the responsibility that goes with it.

TWO KINDS OF OBEDIENCE

There are two kinds of obedience: Active and passive.

Active obedience is when God has a specific task for us to do for Him. When He tells us to "go."

My son Dan graduated from seminary last year, and he was most anxious to find out what God wanted him to do. He and his wife, Kathy, spent much time in prayer seeking God's will. Kathy comes from a close-knit family in Spokane, Washington, so when a position opened up in the northwest it sounded like the right one. Then they heard of another available position, but it was clear across the country in Connecticut. This seemed to be the one God wanted them to accept. It was difficult to follow God's "go" when it meant moving so far away, but as Dan and Kathy prayed about it they felt New England was where they should be.

Sometimes it's hard to follow Jesus in obedience. Yet when we do, we learn that the path which often seemed the most difficult to travel holds the greatest glory. Today God has His hand of love upon Dan and Kathy's lives, and they are living in active obedience.

Abraham exhibited active obedience at its highest point when he took Isaac up to the top of Mount Moriah and laid him on the altar.

There is a second kind of obedience, passive obedience. Passive obedience is when Jesus tells us to stop and be quiet in His presence. When He tells us to come apart before we come apart! When He says, "Stay put." Recently my husband was talking with a college student who had just heard a missionary share the needs of the world. This student felt called to drop out of school in the middle of the year and "Go and serve the Lord *now.*" Harry tried to point out to him that probably God wanted him to stay where he was and finish the education he had just as surely felt God had called him to. It never occurred to the young man that God would tell him to "stay" when there was such a need in the world. He thought the call of the gospel was to go, and to go now.

Isn't this how we often feel? We think, "I must go—I must do—I must say," when God is trying to tell us, "Stop—stay—be quiet." Can you hear God's "stop" through the din of your activity for Him? Think what would have happened if Abraham had failed to hear God's "stop"!

THE PERFECT HEART

Three years ago I was out in California visiting my sister, Marilyn Mead. One afternoon when I was sitting on her sunny patio reading my Bible, God said to me, "I want you to write another book." Writing is difficult for me, and after I finished my last book I thought, "I'll never do that again." The more I thought about writing a book the less it appealed to me. It seemed the bookstores were bulging with millions of unread books. Besides, I couldn't think of one subject to write about. "It's all been said before, Lord. Whatever could I write about?" And He replied, "I want you to write about obedience." I moaned, "No one will want to read that, Lord. Surely You know the 'in' thing today is all this positive thinking and feeling. Obedience sounds so negative. If this is Your idea, You'll have to confirm it for me." Just then my sister came out and said it was time to leave for our luncheon appointment, so the idea was pushed to the back of my mind.

When I returned home a week later I found a letter waiting, thanking me for my book on prayer.

The closing sentence said, "My wife and I would like to suggest you write another book and the subject we suggest you write about is obedience." I can still remember standing in my kitchen reading that letter. It seemed as if time had stopped, and I hardly dared to breathe. I felt much like Moses must have felt when God told him what He expected him to do and Moses said, "But I'm not the person for a job like that!" (Exod. 3:11). Who was I to write about obedience?

But I am learning that all God needs is for us to *want* to be obedient. He does the rest. After three years of studying, reading, and gathering notes, I am writing this book on obedience. And here's the promise He gave me the day I started to write:

> "Listen to what I say!
> My words shall fall upon you
> Like the gentle rain and dew,
> Like rain upon the tender grass,
> Like showers on the hillside.
> I will proclaim the greatness of the Lord.
> How glorious He is!
> He is the Rock. His work is perfect."
> (Deut. 32:1).

I am learning that when God asks us to do something for Him, He intends to give us the ability to do it.

Don't underestimate the absolute generosity of God. He longs to shower us with His blessings and give us the skills to live the obedient Christian life. Our daily prayer must become, "Lord, give me an obedient heart, a heart that is perfect toward You."

God is waiting to bestow this upon us. "For the eyes of the Lord search back and forth across the whole earth, looking for people whose hearts are perfect toward him, so that he can show his great power in helping them" (2 Chron. 16:9).

This doesn't mean God is looking for perfect people. There aren't any. Rather, He is searching, throughout the earth, for those whose hearts are perfect *toward Him.* The cornerstone of the obedient life is this perfect heart *toward God.* Ask Him to give you such a heart, and He will. He takes that little flame of desire and fans it with the breath of His Holy Spirit. "Jesus never gives desires He doesn't mean to fill."[2] The perfect heart looks at Jesus and longs to be like Him.

When our heart is perfect toward God in obedience, we become teachable, self-controlled people who are willing to accept the discipline that comes with learning obedience. Then we want what God wants. We no longer need to experience the seesaw Christian living.

When Dr. Cornelius Van Til, one of the leading Christian apologists of the twentieth century, was asked what he would most like to be remembered for, he said, "I should like to be remembered as one who was faithful to Him 'from whom, through whom and unto whom all things are.'"[3] May this be our desire also.

7 Our Choice

We can choose the sounds we want to listen to; we can choose the taste we want in food, and we should choose to follow what is right (Job 34:3–4).

I was in a hurry to get to Denver where I had a speaking engagement. The right-hand side of the interstate highway was filled with slow drivers, so I stayed in the passing lane. As I looked in the rear-view mirror, I saw a gasoline truck looming up behind me at an enormous speed. "He's a menace to the highway!" I thought. And I took it upon myself to teach him a lesson in proper driving. I clutched the steering wheel and determined not to let him pass. The more he blinked his lights and blew his horn, the more determined I became. Suddenly it had become my calling in life to make a good driver out of him!

This incident later reminded me of a cartoon I had seen. It showed a pleasant-faced man getting up in the morning, singing as he got ready for work, greeting his wife and children with a cheerful kiss. On the way to the garage, he waved to the neighbor and took time to pet the neighborhood cat. But once behind the wheel of his car, this nice man turned into a monster. With a fiendish gleam in his eye, he aimed his car down the street. He cut in and out of drivers, blowing his horn and shouting at everyone in his path. The final scene showed him arriving at work—the car safely parked. Once again he was smiling, greeting the elevator operator with a hearty "Good morning" and tipping his hat to all he met.

I could identify with the man in the cartoon! I am a shy, quiet person who would never dream of trying to teach a truck driver a lesson in safe driving. Why had I chosen to do so that morning? Why did the man in the cartoon choose to let himself become a snarling maniac once he was behind the wheel of his car?

A good place to start practicing the obedient life is in these relatively minor irritations that confront us in daily living. When we get behind the wheel of a car, when a salesperson is rude to us, or when our carefully planned schedule is interrupted, we have the perfect proving ground for obedient living. At these times we must choose, by an act of our will, how we are going to respond.

Two friends were talking recently, and one remarked how the heartaches and sorrows we experience can color our whole life. "Yes," replied the other, "but isn't it great that we get to choose the color?" I had chosen to let that speeding truck driver color my morning a bright, intolerant red.

What color are you painting your life today? Living the obedient Christian life involves a continuous round of personal choices. When we respond to the question, "What is Your will for me now in the midst of this situation," we are choosing the color of our life. Each day we face disappointments and hurts of one degree or another because we live in a lost and fallen world, with lost and fallen people, and we cannot escape the inevitable results. However, God has given us authority to choose the way we will respond to these daily disappointments. We can paint them black, or a soft blue, or even a sunshine yellow. The choice is always ours to make. This is the freedom and responsibility of obedient living.

One weekend I was speaking at a retreat in Estes Park, Colorado. At the close of an evening meeting, an attractive young woman came up to talk to me. The first thing I noticed was the radiant smile that lit up her entire face. Then she told me that five weeks before her four-year-old child had died. She told how during that time of extreme loss and heartbreak she had sensed the steady presence of God. As she walked down that long dark tunnel of sorrow, she knew God was with her. It was as though He had picked her up and carried her through in His loving arms. As she talked to me, the tears rained down her cheeks, but when they touched her smile they seemed to burst into a brilliant rainbow. Somehow, through all the sadness and heartache she had experienced, she had received the strength to choose not to be sucked down into the blackness of despair. Instead, by an act of her will, she had painted her sorrow with the iridescent colors of God's love. And because of this choice, she was able to attend a retreat so soon after her loss and to return home strengthened and nourished by God's love and by the love of the Christian family that surrounded her. I am confident no one at the retreat will forget her. I know I won't. She had chosen to receive the gentle colors of God's healing in the midst of the blackness, and that choice made all the difference in her world.

We do not just drift into the obedient life. It is something we choose. It involves a daily decision to put our lives into the hands of the Almighty. Then our steps are guided by the God who loves us and gave Himself for us and who has a destiny for us. As we choose to live our life in obedience to Him, we discover the dynamic reality that our destiny *is* ordained, and we are free to become all He created us to be.

Because we do have a choice, obedience must have its opposite—disobedience. We can choose not to obey God. We can choose not to hear Him. "They would not obey my rules even though obeying them means life" (Ezek. 20:13). We can become deaf to His voice if we don't want to hear what He is saying.

This happened to me with a dress I bought. When I got home from the store, I realized I shouldn't have bought it. It was too expensive and I didn't need it. Six weeks passed before I had an opportunity to return it, although I knew the store wouldn't give my money back because I recalled seeing a sign above the cash register, "No refunds after thirty days." Because I needed the money and didn't need the dress, I decided to tell them the dress had been a birthday gift. I chose to lie even though I knew it was wrong. The money I would get back seemed more important than obeying God.

When the saleslady asked me when my birthday was, I found myself lying again, saying, "A couple weeks ago." How could I tell her it was ten months ago! As I stood there waiting for the store manager to come, my heart grew cold. I thought, "What am I going to do? I've already told two lies about this dress. What if the manager needs to see my driver's license for identification and discovers my birthday was ten months ago. How can I get out of this dreadful mess?" Having it "my way" was no fun! I was a nervous wreck by the time the saleslady returned. I hastily mumbled something about keeping the dress, shoved it into the bag, and left in a hurry.

When I got back to the car, I asked the Lord to forgive me. I told Him I was sorry I had deliberately closed my ears to what was right. He showed me to what depths I could sink in such a short time. Two lies in less than one minute! That dress now reminds me of the awesome responsibility God has given me in the freedom of choice. I am learning my heart can become hardened to His voice and that I can become spiritually deaf if I continue to deliberately choose not to hear Him.

What kind of Christ-followers are we? We can be like Peter who followed Jesus closely, right up to His death. Or we can be like those who are spoken of in the Gospels where it says, "And they followed afar off." He has left the choice to us.

When I think back over my life, I see specific instances where I knowingly chose to be obedient to God, and I discover two things:

1. how few those times really are
2. what glorious results came about because of my obedience

Joshua told the children of Israel, "Choose you this day whom ye will serve" (Josh. 24:15 KJV). Centuries later we are still confronted with this choice many times daily in the Christian life.

"How long are you going to waver between two opinions? . . . If the Lord is God, *follow* him!" (1 Kings 18:21).

8 The Holy Spirit

Make me walk along the right paths for I know how delightful they really are (Ps. 119:35).

The shortest path to a "religious" nervous breakdown is to try to live the obedient life alone. Attempting to be obedient by sheer will power can leave one a despondent, guilt-ridden "basket case" within three days. It's like the New Year's resolutions made at the beginning of each year; a week later, most are broken and forgotten. In our zeal to be obedient, we join the "clenched-teeth club" and vow our obedience to God until the day we die. But we still end up where Paul did in Romans 7: "It seems to be a fact of life that when I want to do what is right, I inevitably do what is wrong.... In my mind I want to be God's willing servant, but. . . . the old nature that is still inside me loves to sin. Oh, what a terrible predicament I'm in!" (Rom. 7:21–25).

"To cope" has become the key phrase of this decade. We hear things like, "I simply can't cope with this any more," or "I'm trying so hard to cope." The Holy Spirit came to give us the capacity to cope with life.

It is impossible to live the obedient life without the enabling power of the Holy Spirit, and Jesus never intended that we should try. He knew living the obedient life would not be easy and that He was asking something difficult and demanding so He gave us the Holy Spirit to be our helper. When Jesus calls us to a life of 100 percent obedience, He gives us the power to do it.

When Jesus commanded the paralytic to take up his bed and walk, He gave the crippled man the ability to walk. And so it is with us. God commands us to be obedient to Him. Then He gives us the power and ability to obey that command through the Holy Spirit.

HE GOES WITH US

Jesus knows how hard it is to live in today's world with all its hate, dishonesty, and suffering. He understands the hurts and heartbreaks of living together as a family. He knows what it means to be tempted. He knows our struggles. He is not sitting in some far-off heaven shouting commands to us. He understands the loneliness many of us face each day. He lived on this planet for thirty-three years. He, too, once lived on the raw cutting edge of life. He says to us, "Look, I know I'm asking something difficult of you in this obedience. I know your fears and worries. But listen, I have given you the Holy Spirit. He will help you. He will enable you. He will give you the strength to obey." And He takes us by the hand and goes with us.

When our family was young, we took a trip to Germany. We had our guidebook on how to get through Europe on $10.00 a day and were following it meticulously. At one point the book described a good hotel in the particular town we were in, and we were desperately searching for it. We spent a half-hour going around in circles. When we asked for directions, they were given in rapid German or broken English which we couldn't understand. It was getting dark and the children were hungry. Finally, when we stopped for a red light, Harry rolled down the car window and asked the man in the car next to us if he could tell us how to find the hotel. The man didn't speak English, but he recognized the name of the hotel and gave us a huge smile. He beckoned us to follow him. As we wound through the picturesque streets, our fears left us. We trusted this man who was leading us; we rested in his ability to take us to the hotel. He led us right up to the door, smiled, and waved good-by. He hadn't told us how to go; he had *led* us. He went *with us,* and it made all the difference. This is what Jesus does when He asks for our obedience. He gives us the Holy Spirit who goes with us and shows us the way.

There is a difference between God's command and God's invitation. Obedience is something He expects us to do, but His command is always followed by His gracious invitation, "Come now, let's do this together."

When God gives a command to obey, we are anointed by the Holy Spirit to do it. There is no lack of trust in this kind of obedience. The curtain of fear is parted, and in each small, obedient step we can see the joy that comes with it. The moment we step out on our weak, trembling legs of faith and obey we discover the Holy Spirit giving us the strength and ability to obey. "Faith is weakness clinging to the strength of God."

DEPENDENCY ON THE HOLY SPIRIT

Our Christian life moves upon the twin rails of:

1. obedience to God
2. dependency on the Holy Spirit.

It is imperative that these two rails remain parallel at all times. If one gets ahead of the other, disaster will follow. If we major on obedience at the expense of dependency on the Holy Spirit, we will fail. If we major on dependency at the expense of obedience, we will become irresponsible Christians.

The moment we receive Jesus as Savior, the Holy Spirit enters our life. He becomes our guarantee, or seal, that we really do belong to the family of God (2 Cor. 1:22 NIV). Before Pentecost, believers *asked* for the Holy Spirit (Luke 11:13). Since Pentecost, we *receive* Him (Acts 2:38).

Our responsibility is to open our life each day to receive the leading and teaching of the Holy Spirit and to let Him renew every part of our life. Paul tells us we are to "be filled with the Spirit" (Eph. 5:18). The Greek word for "be filled" means to be continuously filled. We choose, in an act of obedience, to surrender our lives anew to Him each day.

Recently when my husband was washing the car, he asked me to hand him the sponge that was in the garage. When I brought it to him, the sponge was stiff, unbending, and dry. After I dropped it into the pail of water, it became soft and pliable. When I lifted it out of the water, it had become so saturated with water that the water literally poured out from every part of it.

This is the way our life should be—filled to over-flowing, saturated with the love and power of the Holy Spirit. Then the rivers of living water, which Jesus promised, can flow from us and touch everyone we come in contact with during the day (John 4:14).

Being filled with the Holy Spirit means that He takes complete possession of our life. It means being continuously filled. It means surrendering anew to Him each day. It means being open and tender to His leading and teaching.

The Holy Spirit brings the mighty power of God into our life. He sweeps in like a strong, rushing wind, and we are given the power to live the life to which God has called us. We have confidence that God's Spirit flows through us twenty-four hours a day. Then our lives become radiant with the glow of the presence of God, and we find an increased desire to grow in the knowledge of the Lord. We long to spend time alone with Him reading the Bible and praying. We are acutely aware of His presence with us moment by moment. God's will and purpose for our life become clear, and we become strengthened as our knowledge of Him increases. The Holy Spirit gives us the wisdom to know what is right and the power to do it.

This obedient, dependent life is one of complete faith and trust.

I gained a better understanding of this as I watched my son Tom and his wife care for their precious baby, Breelyn. When Breelyn was hungry, they fed her. When she was tired, they rocked her to sleep. When she was thirsty, they gave her a drink. When she wanted to be held and cuddled, they hugged her close in their arms. Whatever her needs were, she turned to her parents in utter trust, confident they would be met.

What a beautiful picture of our dependency on the Holy Spirit. When we are afraid, He is our comforter. When we are uncertain which way to go, He is our guide. When we lack knowledge, He is our teacher. When we choose to be obedient, He empowers us to obey. We turn to Him in complete trust and confidence, knowing He will meet our every need.

THE HOLY SPIRIT AS GUIDE

When God speaks to you through the Holy Spirit,

listen carefully to His instructions. If you aren't sure what He said, ask Him to repeat it; He will. He isn't trying to hide anything from you.

Early one afternoon, about a year ago, Harry came home from work and said in a strange tone of voice, "Come and sit down on the couch. I have something to share with you." When we were seated, he cleared his voice and said, "What would you think of moving to Chicago?" Chicago! He *had* to be kidding. How could we leave beautiful Colorado Springs after living there for ten years? He must have gotten his instructions wrong! But as we talked and prayed about it during the next few days, we both felt the Holy Spirit was saying, "Chicago." I must confess, I asked several times during those days, "Lord, are You *sure* You mean Chicago?" (You can ask Him to repeat His instructions if you aren't sure. But once you know what He has asked of you, then do it.) Our move to the Chicago area has been the beginning of a whole new life for us. As each month passes, we see the unfolding of His plan a little more.

There isn't any way we can obey the Holy Spirit's orders if we don't hear them. This is why we must learn to listen. So often I am asked, "How do I know God is talking to me? How do I know it's not just my own thought or idea?" Part of the answer to that question lies in our trust and confidence in God. If we have sought His guidance and sense that He has given it, then we take it on faith and act on it. We have the confidence that if it weren't what He wanted, He would have closed the door. God is not playing games with us. If we ask Him, He will answer just as He promised. He tells us, "My sheep recognize my voice . . . and they follow me" (John 10:27). When you take time to listen to the Holy Spirit, you develop your spiritual ear; you hear His voice and you know it.

When you step out on faith and act upon what you believe He has told you, you become sensitive to His voice. If you have doubts about what you think He told you, check it out with the Bible. God will never tell you to do anything that is contrary to His Word. Use the Ten Commandments as your guide. Or use the two principles of Christian living that were mentioned in an earlier chapter:

1. Does it coincide with my love and commitment to Jesus?
2. Does it coincide with my love and commitment to others?

The obedient Christian is one who spends his or her life listening to the voice of the Holy Spirit and then acting, in faith, upon what has been heard. Desire more of Jesus, more of His love, and more obedience to carry out His will. Look to the Holy Spirit in total dependency to guide and direct. Learn to live in obedience to all He has told you to do and learn to live in dependency upon all He has promised.

Step out on faith, believing that the God of the universe does speak to you.

Obedience Is Learned

Now teach me good judgment as well as knowledge. For your laws are my guide. (Ps. 119:66).

We were sitting by the fire watching the Winter Olympics on television. Dorothy Hamill had just finished her dazzling gold-medal performance. As I watched her glide over the ice so freely and gracefully, I said with a sigh, "I wish I could skate like that." But did I really? Would I want to go through all she had gone through to reach that great moment? The life of total discipline and self-denial? Arising at five o'clock every morning for years to practice? Spending eight hours a day on the ice while her friends were out having a good time? Her entire life centered around skating. No sacrifice was too great. No,

I think what I really meant was that I wished I could skate like Hamill did without having to practice the dedicated discipline that went into it. I would have liked all the rewards of winning a gold medal without the years of practice, self-denial, and hard work.

This can happen in our Christian life as well. We search for ways to become "instant spiritual giants." We hope to get tapped on the head with God's magic wand so we, too, can part the sea or walk on the water. We want the joy of being close to Jesus without the obedience this demands. We assume that because we want to be obedient we will be. But it takes much more than just wanting. True, the wanting needs to be there because it is the seed of desire that is sown in our minds. This seed will eventually be quickened with the power of the Holy Spirit and produce obedience. But first we must be utterly convinced that our goal deserves the discipline and self-denial necessary for achievement. We must know in our heart this is something that deserves our best.

There is no shortcut to living the Christian life, just as there is no shortcut to becoming a gold medalist. We must understand that we learn obedience, and learning obedience must become our goal. While we focus on that goal, we also keep our eyes fixed steadily upon the living One who deserves the obedience He demands. Our total abandonment to obedient living allows us the freedom to become all God created us to be.

D. L. Moody was motivated by the statement, "The world has yet to see what God can do with a person totally yielded to Him," and he set out to be that person. Read his life story and see what God accomplished through him. Hundreds of thousands of people have been touched by his life because he was willing to let God make him all he was created to be.

Jesus called us to be His disciples, to bring the message of salvation to the lost and dying world around us, but we can never be disciples unless we are obedient. The Bible tells us that Jesus learned obedience (Heb. 5:8), and we, too, must learn it. The Holy Spirit is our teacher. Because we know and trust our great Teacher, we are eager to learn.

Our first year as missionaries in Brazil was spent in language school learning Portuguese. One professor stood out above the rest. She was a dedicated teacher who took a personal interest in each student and delighted in our daily progress. She led us day by day, a step at a time, deeper into the language. She made us realize how important it was that we learn Portuguese if we wanted the freedom of sharing our lives with the Brazilians. She constantly impressed upon us how frustrating and lonely our lives in Brazil would be without the freedom of speaking the language. She convinced us of the desperate necessity of discipline and self-denial. At all times, she had our best interest at heart. Her demands for perfection were not designed to make us miserable or to ruin our lives, but to enable us to live a free and productive life among the Brazilians. When we graduated at the end of the year, we were able to speak Portuguese fluently.

This is exactly the way it is with our Teacher, the Holy Spirit. Because we love and trust Him so completely, we are open to learning obedience from Him. And as a result, our life becomes free and productive. We become all He created us to be; we become that luminous glow of the presence of God in our world.

There is a principle of life which says that we learn by doing. That's the only way I learned Portuguese. I could have sat in that class all year and never learned a word if I hadn't started speaking the language. I had to study and practice, make mistakes, and try again and again. And this is the way we learn obedience. We only learn by doing. We can read every book ever written about obedience, we can study God's Word and find out all the great things He taught about obedience, but until we actually step out, in the power of the Holy Spirit, and obey we will never learn. *We learn to obey by obeying.*

Our goal, or our dream, in the Christian life must be 100 percent obedience. If only we would learn this when we come to Jesus, we wouldn't have a world full of pigmy Christians. The obedient life is not just for the spiritual giants (whatever that means). The call for obedience is to all who have put their faith and trust in Jesus Christ as Savior. The moment we give our life to Him is the moment we must begin our obedient life. We continue to learn and obey until we meet Him face to face.

One of the gracious marks of obedient Christians is that they are teachable. It's difficult to be with people who know everything, isn't it? They seem so superior and abrasive. My husband meets with a young college student each week for Bible study. Every time Harry meets with Brad Mason he comes home with a light step and a happy sparkle in his eye because Brad is teachable. He wants to learn. He once told Harry, "I just want to sit at your feet and learn everything you know." The obedient Christian is one who has a teachable spirit, a gentle spirit, and who walks humbly with God. The obedient Christian is one who prays daily for an obedient heart, a heart that is perfect toward God.

THE BIBLE

The ability to obey is not learned on the battlefield of life; it is learned by being alone with God. It is through the reading of the Bible that we learn about God, what He is like and how He expects us to live. Obedience is then putting God's Word into action. "Obey me and live! Guard my words as your most precious possession" (Prov. 7:2).

A friend said recently, "I would read my Bible more, but it seems like a waste of time. I forget everything I've read five minutes later." I've felt this way too sometimes, haven't you? But I am learning that we don't have to remember or understand everything we read. It's through the reading that the Holy Spirit takes the living Word and implants it in our heart, in our subconscious mind. We are *always* nourished spiritually through the reading of His Word whether we *feel* like it or not. It is *always* a life-giving source to strengthen us and teach us the way we should go.

We may not remember everything we read in our Bible, but we have confidence that our great God has ministered to us spiritually and that we have been built up in the love and knowledge of His Word. It is the devil who tells us that reading the Bible is a waste of time when we don't remember all we've read. We cannot permit him to deceive us in this important area. It is vital that we spend time in God's Word each day if we are going to be obedient.

Let me share a simple plan that helps me in reading my Bible. Before I begin, I ask the Holy Spirit to open my eyes and my heart to the reading of God's Word. Then, with pencil in hand, I mark the verses which speak to me.

If there is a promise that seems meant for me that day, I jot the date down in the margin with a note about why it encouraged me. I put a "p" after every promise and claim it for my own.

When I come to something God says to do, I put a small plus sign (+) in the margin. Then I look for an opportunity *that day* to put that plus into practice.

If I come across a verse that tells me something not to do, I put a minus sign (–) in the margin. Then I ask the Holy Spirit to keep that minus from creeping unnoticed into my life.

Before I close my Bible, I take a moment to pray over each item I have marked. I thank Him for the promise, commit all the pluses to His care, and ask for strength to protect me from the minuses. This has made my Bible reading personal and alive with meaning.

Reading the Bible is an essential part of the Christian life. There can be no lasting obedience without it. Read it, meditate upon it, memorize it, and make it a part of your very being. God will bless you for it. He will open the eyes of your understanding, and your life will take on the luminous glow of His presence.

Then you can say with David, "Your words are a flashlight to light the path ahead of me, and keep me from stumbling" (Ps. 119:105).

PRAYER

We cannot be close to Jesus or minister to the needs of others unless we are praying Christians. Prayer is being with Jesus; it is walking with Him and talking with Him. It is fellowship with the living God of the universe. Prayer is conversation between two friends who love and understand each other.

As we spend time in prayer daily, we find a new hunger and thirst to be close to God in obedience. Then this time alone with Him becomes the most important thing we do during the day. There is no way we can ignore the Source of our strength and power, Jesus Christ, and live an obedient life.

"The secret of true obedience . . . is the clear and close personal relationship to God. All our attempts after full obedience will be a failure until we get access to His abiding fellowship. It is God's holy presence abiding with us that keeps us from disobeying Him."[1]

Learn what it means to be alone with God in prayer, for when we have been *with Him,* our love for Him produces obedience.

A COMMON MISTAKE

One of the greatest mistakes we can make is to say, "Lord, I'll be obedient to You for the next twenty years," or "I'll be obedient the rest of my life." God doesn't ask for that. He asks that we live the obedient life *today.* It's always one day at a time with the Lord. He knows and understands us far more than we know and understand ourselves. When Peter said so fervently, "Lord, I'll *never* forsake You," the Lord knew Peter's heart. He knew Peter didn't intend to forsake Him, but He also knew that, "In ourself dwelleth no good thing" (Rom. 7:18). And with great love and understanding He turned to Peter and said, "Oh, dear Peter, before the night is over you will have denied Me three times." Don't tell the Lord you'll obey Him forever and ever. He isn't asking for that. He is asking for obedience today. This moment. In *this* situation. God told the children of Israel to gather fresh manna every morning and to gather just enough for that day, not enough for a whole week, and certainly not for forty years. It's always morning by morning with the Lord. He sends us out a day at a time to do a specific task for Him, and each morning we stop by His office to pick up our orders. A lifetime of obedience is more than we can take on, and God understands this.

Three years ago our son-in-law, Marc, learned he

had diabetes. The doctor told him, "No more doughnuts, no more cakes, no more pies or anything with sugar *for the rest of your life!"* Talk about a tough life sentence, that was it! It was enough to make the strongest person shudder with gloom. A lifetime without "goodies" and with daily insulin shots seemed more than Marc could bear. Yet he is learning the freedom that comes with being able to say, "*Today* I can go without a doughnut or candy bar. *Today* I can take my insulin shot and be thankful for the strength it brings." Marc is learning the discipline of living his life one day at a time.

Jesus never expects us to do anything for "as long as we live." It's always this day, this moment, this situation with the Lord. "So don't be anxious about tomorrow, God will take care of your tomorrow too. Live one day at a time" (Matt. 6:34).

The Christian life involves both an eternal commitment to God and a moment by moment walk with Him, morning by morning, day by day. This is the joy of obedience.

Facing Guilt and Failure

I would have despaired and perished unless your laws had been my deepest delight. I will never lay aside your laws, for you have used them to restore my joy and my health (Ps. 119:92).

I marvel at the patience of a baby learning to walk. These little ones haven't been in the world long enough to know that after several failures, human beings give up. Our granddaughter, Breelyn, was visiting us when she took her first tottering steps. As her mother helped her get her balance, Breelyn stood unsteadily for a brief moment, then ventured out slowly, taking one wobbling step and then another.

Her daddy was a few paces away on the floor, holding out his arms to catch her. She fell several times along her little pathway, but she always got up and tried again, keeping her eyes fixed upon her father as she tottered across the room. The closer she got to him, the more excited she became. Her eyes were dancing, and with a happy smile of triumph she collapsed into his arms with peals of laughter. During the ten days they visited us, she must have fallen hundreds of times, but she never gave up.

When Breelyn fell, her parents didn't punish her, nor did they have a big stick to prod her on. They didn't say, "Well, that did it, Breelyn. You've fallen six times in the last five minutes. We're finished with you!" Instead, they were there to encourage her and help her back on her feet each time she fell. And Breelyn never stopped trying. She didn't say, "It hurts too much to fall. I think I'll just crawl through life." And it never occurred to her that her parents would not be there to help and encourage her. Isn't this the way it is with our heavenly Father? "If you, then, though you are evil, know how to give good gifts to your children, how much more will your Father in heaven give good gifts to those who ask him!" (Matt. 7:11 NIV).

Often when talking to people, I hear something like this: "Well, I tried to live the Christian life, but I just kept blowing it." So they give up. They think God is angry with them, that He's up there with a big stick ready to punish them every time they fall. As a result, they end up crawling through their Christian life.

They never experience the delight of walking with God or the thrill of running and skipping, full of the abundant life He came to give (John 10:10).

The obedient life springs from a simple, childlike faith in Jesus Christ. He told us, "I tell you the truth, unless you change and become like little children, you will never enter the kingdom of heaven" (Matt. 18:3 NIV). In our obedient walk towards God, we take one small tottering step of faith and then another one, all the while keeping our eyes fixed steadily upon Jesus and His smile of encouragement. When we fall, as we will, He reaches out and picks us up and sets us gently upon our feet. And we try once more. Soon we discover we can walk through a whole hour in obedience to Him. If we fall later on, we don't throw a spiritual temper tantrum or abandon our Christian life; rather, we allow Jesus to pick us up again—and again—and again. We hear His voice of assurance, "I'll be here to pick you up each time you fall." ("I will never, *never,* fail you nor forsake you" Heb. 13:5).

GOD SEES THE HEART

How do we feel when we see one of our children trying so hard to be good? Aren't we filled with tenderness and joy, even if they fail? We love them for trying, and we stand behind their desire with encouragement and love. God acts the same way with us, His children. He knows the intent of our heart, and He counts it as obedience. He sees our sincere love for Him which motivates our desire to obey, and He rejoices. He loves us in our weakness and He loves us in our strength. He loves us when we obey Him and He loves us when we disobey.

Read the life of King David in the Bible and see how often he utterly failed God. Yet God refers to him as obedient. God even used David's obedience as an example to his son Solomon (1 Kings 3:14). David had a heart that was open and tender to the Holy Spirit. He was filled with remorse when he sinned, and he repented after each failure. (Read Psalm 51.) It was always David's heart God saw when He looked at him, and He called David obedient. "Man looks at the outward appearance, but the Lord looks at the heart" (1 Sam. 16:7 NIV).

Look at each failure and note what you can learn from it. (One of the greatest mistakes you can make is to learn nothing from your mistakes!) Confess it. Acknowledge it as sin and offer it up to God. Ask Him to forgive you and to cleanse you from that particular thing. (He will.) Don't permit your failure to obey yesterday to spoil your obedience today. The most important move you can make is the move you make after you have failed Him.

We need to remember that we will fail from time to time in our obedient walk with God. The devil will be quick to move in at that time, in the midst of our failure, and attempt to turn the joy of obedience into guilt and despair. It is imperative that we understand that we are in a battle with a deadly enemy who is out to destroy us.

SATAN'S FAVORITE WEAPONS

There are three ways in which the devil delights to attack believers in their desire to be obedient. His first method of attack is *compromise*. Compromise is one of Satan's favorite words. "Come now," he whispers, "you can afford to wink a little at this. After all, you're not perfect, and no one expects you to be. Not even God!" And before we know what's happened, we are living a compromising, weak, watered-down, meaningless Christian life. We must recognize that there can be absolutely no compromise in our obedient walk with God. Satan is aware of our frailties, and he will hurl the darts of compromise at us again and again, attempting to wound us. Ask the Holy Spirit to keep you alert to the danger of compromising your obedient walk with God, and He will.

The second method of attack the devil uses is to question *motives*. If we are being obedient, he moves in with this clever deception: "Look," he says, "your motives aren't pure. God doesn't want this kind of polluted obedience."

Take the example from the life of my friend Betty. Betty's neighbor had just returned home from the hospital so Betty thought it would be nice to bake a chocolate cake for the family. She wanted to do this for the Lord and for her neighbor. But while she was getting the ingredients out to bake the cake, the devil came and whispered, "You know you're not really doing this for the Lord. You're doing it so your neighbor will say, 'Isn't Betty nice?'" The longer Betty thought about this, the more she realized it was partly true. She did want her neighbor to think she was nice. But she also wanted to do it for the Lord. It was the kind of thing He would do if He were here. However, she decided she should not bake the cake because her motives were not "pure." When Betty told me about this, she said she felt sad because:

1. She didn't make the cake for her neighbors.
2. She must not be a good Christian because she wanted someone to think she was nice.

As a result:

1. The family across the street missed out on a chocolate cake and an experience of Christian love in action.
2. Betty felt guilty and unworthy of God's love.

We seldom do anything with absolutely pure motives. There is usually a bit of self in every good thing that is accomplished in life, and the devil loves to capitalize on this by implanting the idea that before we can attempt anything for God, our motives must be absolutely pure.

When we lived in Brazil, Harry had to return to the States for six weeks on mission business. Because I knew I would be lonely while he was gone, I decided to work on some special project. I had brought all my flannelgraph Bible stories with me from the States, hoping I could use them with the Brazilian children, and I decided this was a good time to start. I got them out with eager anticipation, tucked them under my arm, and went calling at each house in the neighborhood. I introduced myself and explained that I wanted to invite the children to a weekly Bible story time at my house.

The Lord blessed that little class in an amazing way. No one had ever paid any attention to those children. No one had ever told them a story or taught them a song. How can I describe the joy I had in being the first person to tell them about the love of Jesus?

One by one, down through the years, those children came to my gate and said, "Doña Hopie, I want to invite Jesus into my heart. Please will you help me." What a ministry God gave me! I cherish it as one of the most important things I have ever done. Yet it did not stem from "pure motives."

I had started that class because I was lonesome while Harry was away. I had wanted a special project to carry me over until he came home. Of course, I also wanted the children to hear about the love of Jesus; I strongly believe in the importance of giving children the message of salvation at a young age. Many times during that first year people told me what a wonderful work was being done for the children, and I felt guilty. I knew I had begun the work with mixed motives. But God knew that too! Nothing is hidden from Him. And He took those motives, *as they were,* and used them for His honor and glory. He knew my heart, and He saw my sincere love for Him and the children. That's all He needed. How sad it would have been had I let the devil keep me from teaching that Bible class because I didn't have absolutely pure motives!

When you feel God is asking you to do something for Him, do it. Don't sit around and wait until your motives are pure because most likely they never will be. Satan tries to keep us from living the obedient life by deceiving us into thinking anything we do for God must be done only with 100 percent pure motives. And the angels weep over the lost opportunities.

Satan's third attack weapon is *fear*. The moment we tell God we want to be obedient, we are afraid He will rub His hands together with glee and say, "Now let's see, what's the most dreadful thing I could ask her to do. Oh, yes, she hates spiders and enjoys home. I think I'll ask her to leave all for the jungles of Africa. That should do just fine for a starter!" We are afraid if we give God half a chance, He will move in and completely ruin our lives.

Our ideas are so distorted. God knows us better than we will ever know ourselves. When we give our lives to Him, in obedience, He says, "Now I can help her live life to the fullest. Now I can help her become all I created her to be." There is no guilt or fear in the kind of life Jesus came to give.

Some Christians are engulfed in guilt and anxiety if all their time is not spent serving the Lord or reading the Bible. They feel guilty if they play golf or spend a day at the beach. They mistakenly assume that if they would ask God how they should use their free time He would always say, "Go read your Bible! Go pray! Go talk to your neighbor!" Now He may well say those things. But He also might say, "Well, why don't you spend the evening sitting by the fire, eating popcorn, and reading a good mystery" (Would you then shake your head in disbelief and say, "What—Lord, was that You?")

We forget that He knows the hectic kind of world we live in. We forget that He created a beautiful world full of things that demonstrate how much He wants us to enjoy life. He created us with the need to relax and have fun, to laugh and shout and skip with joy.

Don't permit the devil to deceive you into thinking you must always be doing something "spiritual" or "productive." Remember, God created laughter and joy. And God made the snowflakes and raindrops, the fresh air and warm sunshine, the mountains and oceans. Everything that is beautiful and lovely comes from Him, and He delights in setting His creation free and filling us with joy. Jesus Christ is the author of life.

Satan, on the other hand, is the author of death.

> *The devil is the murderer of the whole human race. The devil leads to death. . . . The devil murders goodness, chastity, honour, honesty, beauty, all that makes life lovely. The devil murders peace of mind and happiness and even love. The devil is essentially a killer. . . . The devil characteristically loves falsehood. The false word, the false thought, the twisting of truth, the lie belong to the devil.*[1]

We must get this clear in our mind—the devil is out to destroy. He's out to destroy you, your family, and the entire world. He is prowling the earth today as a savage lion seeking to destroy everyone in his path. "Be careful—watch out for attacks from Satan, your great enemy. He prowls around like a hungry, roaring lion, looking for some victim to tear apart" (1 Peter 5:8).

If you want to see what the devil produces, look at a young person whose life has been slowly drained from him through the empty promise of drugs. Satan is always the great deceiver and destroyer of life. He takes our sincere desire to live an obedient life and twists and turns it into a thing of guilt, fear, and pride. He is the master of destruction, making evil from goodness and death from life.

My husband and I saw Satan's death-producing results recently in the life of a friend. This man and Harry had attended seminary together, and he later became the pastor of a large church in the South. A few weeks ago our friend called us. He was in Chicago and wanted to see us. We had not seen him in eight years and looked forward to spending time with him.

When the doorbell rang, instead of hearing Harry's happy voice in greeting, I heard him say in anguish, "What's wrong—what happened to you?" And our friend stumbled into the living room.

In halting whispers, he began to share the tragedy of his life. His church had grown, and God had blessed the work beyond all his dreams. They had an enormous missionary budget, and people around the world were being touched with the gospel.

He had a lovely wife and three teen-age children.

But down through the years, he had been slowly destroyed through an uncontrolled spirit of lust. As a result, he had had affairs with various members of his church. A few months ago, it had come out in the open. His wife and children faced the incredible heartbreak in disbelief. Everyone in his church found out about his double life. The entire city read about it for weeks in the newspaper.

As we listened to our friend's story, our hearts broke with sadness. There sat a shell—an empty, broken, shattered man. Once again Satan had succeeded in making evil from goodness and death from life. It reminded me of a story I read recently.

> *There is a terrible story about the experience of an artist who was painting the picture of the Last Supper. It was a great picture and it took him many years to paint it. He went out to find a model for the face of Christ and he found a young man with a face of such transcendent loveliness and purity that he painted him as Jesus. Bit by bit the picture was filled in and one after another of the disciples was painted. There came the day when he needed a model for Judas whose face he had left to the last. He went out and searched in the lowest haunts of the city and in the dens of vice. At last he found a man with a face so depraved and vicious that he took him as the model for the face of Judas. When the sittings were at an end the man said to the artist, "You painted me before." "Surely not," said the artist. "O yes" said the man, "and the last time you painted me, you painted me as Christ."*[2]

Don't let the devil rob you of your life! Don't let him twist your dreams and goals around for his purposes. Don't let him harden your heart that is open and tender to the leading of the Holy Spirit. Don't let him turn your longing for obedience into a guilt-trip. Don't let him rob you of all God has for you—of all He created you to be. Claim God's promise each day: "The one who is in you is greater than the one who is in the world" (1 John 4:4 NIV). This is a promise to you from the eternal God who must be obedient to His Word. He is greater than any power of Satan, and He will have the victory in your life if you let Him.

Scripture gives us two classic examples of people who utterly failed God, Peter and Judas. Both were His disciples, and both failed Christ in His time of greatest need. Peter denied he even knew Jesus, and Judas betrayed Him with a kiss. But what they did with their failure made all the difference in the world, an eternal difference. Peter faced his failure; he confessed it and went out and wept bitterly. He accepted the fact that he would have to start his life all over again and that he had to start it from the *point of his failure.* God gave Peter the forgiveness and strength he needed, and Peter went on to become one of the greatest Christians the world has ever known.

Judas also failed the Lord. He also denied Him. But Judas's failure ended in tragic defeat because he was destroyed by it. He went out and hung himself.

Jesus stands before us in the midst of our sin and failure, no matter how great or small it may be, and He whispers, "My peace I give you" (John 14:27

NIV). He doesn't give us a lecture on how to be good. He doesn't preach a three-point sermon on how miserable we are. He sees our heart, and He knows we love Him. He knows we long to obey Him. And seeing our failure, He loves us. He offers His forgiveness, paid for with His own blood on the cross. He stands before us in the midst of our sin, shows us the nail prints in His hands, and gently says, "I paid for your failure. I paid for your sin and your disobedience. I paid for your rebellious spirit. I paid for it all on the cross. Now come, I give you My peace."

Regardless of what you may have done, God never stops loving you. He sees beyond your mixed motives and confusion of compromise. He sees the flickering flame of your obedience and fans it into a glowing light for His glory. When you understand this, you can be filled with joy, the fullness of joy about which the Bible speaks. You can have victory and the abundant life He came to give.

Take your eyes off your failure, gloom, and guilt and fix them steadily upon Jesus who stands before you. See yourself as God sees you, clothed in the righteousness of His dear Son. Hold before your eyes the lovely picture of all He created you to be. Contemplate the beauty of your life *as God sees it.* See yourself as all you are becoming in Him as you live the victorious, obedient life.

The Great Adventure

Happy are those who are strong in the Lord, who want above all else to follow your steps. When they walk through the Valley of Weeping it will become a place of springs where pools of blessing and refreshment collect after rains! They will grow constantly in strength (Ps. 84:5–7).

My husband is a dreamer, but he has a way of making his dreams come true. After we had been married a few years, Harry announced he was going to take the entire family to Europe before he was thirty-five. I must admit this was met with great skepticism on my part. Harry was a recent seminary graduate and worked for Young Life earning $200.00 a month—when we got it. Those were the days when our monthly check could be all of $1.65! So you see, dreams of ocean liners and romantic trips through Europe seemed a bit far-fetched.

Somehow, through the years, Harry saved the necessary money, and by the time he was thirty-five, he and I and our three children were on a beautiful luxury liner bound for Europe. We traveled through Europe and ended up studying with Francis Schaeffer in Switzerland for six life-changing months. We had no idea at the time how significant this adventure would prove. Our years in Brazil were a direct result of our time in Europe, and this in turn led to the opening of Young Life in many other countries around the world.

The obedient Christian life is filled with adventure and challenge. It is full of surprises and unexpected encounters. It's the adventure of experiencing events that were not written into our daily schedule. Remember, an adventure isn't really an adventure unless a risk is involved, some element of the unknown. It's the risk that turns an ordinary event into a memorable adventure. Are you willing to take risks? Does stepping out on some uncharted path fill you with anticipation?

I like the verse Harry copied down in the front of the journal we kept while living in Brazil.

I will not follow where the path may lead,
but I will go where there is no path,
and I will leave a trail.

I pray none of us will ever be satisfied with living a safe, secure, protected Christian life. I hope as obedient Christians we won't be afraid of the unknown. There are so many Christians who seem content to be one of the status-quo—to blend in and merge with the crowd. They don't want to "rock the boat" or "make any waves" or do anything for God that is daring or different.

Where do we get the idea that the Christian life is "safe"? That it is nothing more than a warm, fuzzy security blanket or a crutch to support a meek and mild philosophy? We certainly don't get this from the Bible or from the life of Jesus. A Christian is one who is called out into the midst of the battle of life. Jesus taught us to pick up our cross, not our crutch! He said if we want to be Christ's-one, we must "drink the cup I drink" (Mark 10:38 NIV). All of His disciples drank of it, and all of them, except John, were martyred. None of them shrank from life, clutching frantically for security. Instead, they boldly followed Jesus down the uncharted pathway of life. As a result, they were vibrant and alive with the joy of living. There wasn't anything stuffy or dull or ordinary about Jesus, or His message, or His disciples.

> *The people who hanged Christ never, to do them justice, accused Him of being a bore—on the contrary; they thought Him too dynamic to be safe. It has been left for later generations to muffle up that shattering personality and surround Him with an atmosphere of tedium. We have very*

efficiently pared the claws of the Lion of Judah, certified Him "meek and mild," and recommended Him as a fitting household pet for pale curates and pious old ladies. To those who knew Him, however, He in no way suggested a milk-and-water person: they objected to Him as a dangerous firebrand. True, He was tender to the unfortunate, patient with honest inquirers, and humble before Heaven; but He insulted respectable clergymen by calling them hypocrites; He referred to King Herod as "That fox"; He went to parties in disreputable company and was looked upon as a "gluttonous man and a wine-bibber, a friend of publicans and sinners"; He assaulted indignant tradesmen and threw them and their belongings out of the temple . . . He showed no proper deference for wealth and social-position; when confronted with neat dialectical traps, He displayed a paradoxical humour that affronted serious-minded people, and He retorted by asking disagreeably searching questions that could not be answered by rule of thumb. He was emphatically not a dull man in His human lifetime, and (since) He was God, there can be nothing dull about God either. But He had "a daily beauty in His life that made us ugly," and officialdom felt that the established order of things would be more secure without Him. So they did away with God in the name of peace and quietness. . . .

So that is the official story—the tale of the time when God was the underdog and got beaten, when He submitted to the conditions He had laid down and became a man like the men He had made, and the men He had made broke Him and killed Him. This is the dogma we find so dull—this terrifying drama.[1]

If we can find this boring and dull, then what do we consider exciting and stimulating?

IN TOUCH WITH REALITY

Living the obedient Christian life means being in touch with reality at all times. It means facing life head on, not hiding from it. It means running to help people with problems, not running from them.

Recently I read a frightening statement. It said less than 5 percent of all Christians have ever personally shared Jesus Christ with another person. Yet we say He is the most important One in all the world to us; we wonder how we could live even an hour without Him. We say we love Him, we love His church, and we love one another. But somehow we are afraid to step out and take the risk of sharing Him with others. We are afraid we may not be able to answer all their questions. We are afraid we'll be offensive. And as a result, 95 percent of us go through life without telling anyone about Jesus.

One troubled Christian told me, "You know, Hope, I don't know one person who doesn't know Jesus as Savior." All her friends and acquaintances were Christians. When I asked her why she thought this was so, she said, "Perhaps it's because I'm too active in Christian things. I go to church on Sunday and attend two Bible studies during the week. My husband and I belong to a weekly sharing group. I guess I'm just so busy with Christians I never get a chance to meet anyone else or see what's going on in the world."

I think her story is typical of many Christians today: church on Sunday, Bible study on Tuesday, prayer meeting on Wednesday, and missionary circle on Thursday. On Friday night we have a good time of Christian sharing with "the group." As a result, we're gorging ourselves on spiritual food while all around us multitudes are dying for a few crumbs. We sat down at the banquet table the day we received Jesus as Savior, and we haven't gotten up since!

It reminds me of the wedding Harry and I were invited to in India. The reception took place in the grand ballroom of the finest hotel in the country. Never had we seen such a display of wealth. The women were dressed in the finest embroidered silks and satins. Diamonds and rubies and emeralds adorned every finger, forehead, ears and nose. Their arms were laden with bracelets of gold and precious jewels. No words can adequately describe the wealth that was contained in that one room.

Twelve long tables were weighed down with an endless supply of every kind of exotic food: peacock, quail, pheasant, turkey, chicken, and lamb of every imaginable cut; magnificent golden trays of tropical fruit that had been flown in from all over the world; sparkling fountains of drinks sent shimmering strands of liquid into the air, only to fall into waiting golden goblets.

A few steps outside the door, the fetid stench of death filled the humid air. We could see emaciated, shrunken faces pressed against the windows. They stared with vacant, unbelieving eyes, as though unable to comprehend what they saw. And the people inside continued eating, drinking, and laughing, unseeing and uncaring, deaf and blind to the deplorable needs surrounding them.

It was a horrible experience for Harry and me. After half an hour, we went to our host and asked to be excused. We left shaken with revulsion and an ache so deep that it still brings a stab of pain every time we speak of it.

I believe this must be somewhat how God and all the witnesses of heaven feel when they look down and see twentieth century Christians. We are clothed in the spotless robes of the righteousness of Jesus Christ; we are dripping with the precious jewels of the Word of God; we are covered with the diamonds of good Bible teaching and the rubies of Christian fellowship; we abound with the emeralds of Christian literature. Year after year we sit around the banquet table of spiritual food, gorging ourselves until we are obese, frantically trying to cram in more. And a few steps away the stench of a lost and dying world rises up to the very gates of heaven. The angels shed tears of disbelief, and the great crowd of witnesses turns away in abhorrence. We hold in our jeweled hands the answer to the desperate needs of the world, and we don't care. We don't see. We, too, are deaf and blind and oblivious to the profound grief of the lost world around us.

In our continual search for another "spiritual

high," we have ignored the call of Jesus to go into all the world and preach the gospel to *every* person. We've closed our eyes to the fact that this means us. It's more comfortable to think of it as the pastor's job or the missionary's calling. We've closed our ears to God's universal call that all who claim the name of Jesus are commanded to share the glorious treasure of salvation with those who are without. There is no excuse for not obeying this supreme command. Jesus has called us to drink from the cup from which He drank. He has called us to live a life of hard reality in service to others. He has called us to bring hope to the hopeless and to bind up the broken-hearted. He has called us to ease the suffering of the hungry and wounded and to care for the dying. Our prayer must be the one Saint Francis of Assisi prayed daily:

> *Not to be consoled, but to console,*
> *Not to be understood, but to understand*
> *Not to be loved, but to love.*

THE COURAGE OF ADVENTURE

God never promised that the obedient life would be easy, comfortable, or restful. It is not. The obedient life requires courage and a sense of adventure. Today will be different from yesterday. Today we may talk to someone we have never talked to before. We will be open and sensitive to the needs of the person working next to us. We will serve others instead of waiting to be served. A radiant glow will light up the darkness that surrounds us. Being obedient is not always the easy way, but it is always the best.

There will be times when our obedience demands unbelievable courage. The courageous person is not one who says, "I'm not afraid of anything." William Barclay says that courage is not the absence of fear. When your heart is pounding, your hands are cold, and you're deathly afraid, yet you go ahead and do it—that's courage.

I remember when Harry started his first Young Life club thirty-four years ago. When he arrived at the house where the meeting was to be held, he was so afraid that he had to walk around the block three times before he could go in. That's courage!

Let me share a couple of times from my life when courage replaced fear. They may not seem like such courageous acts to you, but because I am a shy, quiet person, they took enormous courage. I wanted to volunteer as a Red Cross Grey Lady so I could visit the patients in a nearby nursing home. The first day I began my duties, I was afraid and nervous. I wondered how I could start conversations with people I didn't even know. But it wasn't long before I realized what an adventure the Lord had given me with endless opportunities to love and serve others.

It took courage to start my first little Bible-story hour for neighborhood children in Seattle. I worked hard on the lessons and was terribly nervous to stand up at the flannelgraph board and tell them the stories. Yet God used that to touch so many young lives, including my own two boys. And then He used it again with the children in Brazil.

The first time I was asked to speak to adults was

to a group of officers' wives at the Air Force Academy. I was an absolute "basket case" for three weeks before the meeting. As I drove to the Academy that morning, I kept wishing I would have a mild heart attack, or *something!* As I was being introduced, my hands were icy cold and my heart was pounding so loud I was sure everyone could hear it. Yet that was a beginning of a whole new ministry for me.

The first time we do anything often takes a great amount of courage. But when we look back, we see how God gave us the needed strength and how others were touched with the love of Jesus. Don't let the lack of courage keep you from stepping out and helping those around you. Don't settle for a life of ease in your Christian life. Accept the daring, challenging, adventuresome life God has for you. When you do, you discover a new love affair with life. A new zest for living will invade your being. You won't go aimlessly through one day after the other marking time. You will be alive with the joy of living and your daily question will become, "Lord, what do You have for me to do today for You?"

You discover a new sensitivity in your life which will point to the hurts and needs of those nearest you. You will yearn to help wipe away the tears from every eye. You see the world with new eyes and a new heart. The ability to see the world *as it is* is perhaps one of the greatest adventures of all in the obedient life. Jesus tells us if we give even a cup of cold water in His name it is the same as if we had personally given Him a drink (Matt. 10:42).

"For I was hungry and you gave me something to eat, I was thirsty and you gave me something to drink, I was a stranger and you invited me in, I needed clothes and you clothed me, I was sick and you looked after me, I was in prison and you came to visit me." And when the people asked Him when they had done these things for Him, He answered, "Whatever you did for one of the least of these brothers of mine, you did for me" (Matt. 25:35–40 NIV).

This beautiful story has been told about Martin of Tours:

> *He was a Roman soldier, and a Christian. One cold winter day, as he was entering a city, a beggar stopped him and asked him for alms. Martin had no money but the beggar was blue and shivering with cold. Martin gave what he had—he took off his soldiers coat, worn and frayed as it was, he cut it in two and gave half of it to the beggar man. That night he had a dream. In it he saw the heavenly places and all the angels and Jesus in the midst of them; and Jesus was wearing half of a Roman soldier's cloak. One of the angels said to Him, "Master, why are you wearing that battered old cloak? Who gave it to you?" And Jesus answered softly, "My servant Martin gave it to me."*[3]

12 Discovery of Joy

So rejoice in him, all those who are his, and shout for joy, all those who try to obey him (Ps. 32:11).

I have a special friend in Brazil. Her name is Doña Jessé. I first met her after I had been studying the Bible with her teen-age daughter, Lourdes, for over a year. One afternoon when we had finished our study, Lourdes said, "Hope, would you come to my house next week and meet my mother? I want her to know Jesus the way I do."

The following week on a sultry summer afternoon I walked to Lourdes' house. The Brazilian sun was at its highest point in the sky, and most people had taken cover in their houses so the red dirt road was quiet and desolate. Lourdes was waiting for me in the front yard, and it was a relief to go into her house out of the sun. The house consisted of three tiny rooms. Each was filled with neatly made beds to take care of the thirteen children and three adults who lived there. Doña Jessé came out to meet me and took me into a small room where we sat on one of the beds to visit. She was thirty-seven years old, but she looked seventy. Her legs were knotted with protruding veins the size of golf balls, and there was a sad, hopeless look in her eyes. Her husband was a thin, tubercular man who worked hard to earn $90.00 a month making bricks.

After we drank our small cups of cafezinho, Doña Jessé turned to me with a tiny spark of hope in her eyes and said, "Would you please tell me how I can know Jesus the way my daughter does?" And there I was, faced with the greatest joy on earth, sharing the Good News of Jesus Christ with another person. I'm sure the angels were singing in that tiny Brazilian bedroom as Doña Jessé was born into the family of God. We set up a weekly time for Bible study, and our times together became some of the most precious times of my life. As I watched Doña Jessé grow in the love and knowledge of the Lord, I saw a transformation take place in her life that could only come from God. Her face became alive with the joy of the Lord. A twinkle was added to her eyes, and she had an insatiable hunger to learn all she could about God's Word.

A year later when I entered the back door of Doña Jessé's little house, I sensed something was different. She met me with a weary look of exhaustion and told me what had happened. Six days earlier her sister from the north had moved in with her. With her came her ten children and they all had terrible cases of trench-mouth. As a result, over half of Doña Jessé's thirteen children had come down with it too. The beds in the three stuffy rooms were filled with sick children. All had burning fevers and mouths swollen with infected sores. As I looked at the tired, worn woman in front of me, I was filled with overwhelming sadness. Twenty-seven people were living in that house—most of them terribly sick. She had meals to prepare three times a day on the small wood-burning stove, and endless demands required her attention.

I said quietly, "Doña Jessé, how are *you* doing in the midst of all this?" And as long as I live, I will never forget her response. Her face suddenly broke out in a radiant smile, and she said, "Right here, in my heart, everything is full of peace. I get up in the morning at 4:30 before anyone else is awake. I come out here and sit at the table and read my Bible and pray, and *I thank God for all His many blessings to me!*" As I looked around at the hopelessness of her situation, I couldn't see even one blessing. Yet she had a whole list!

Doña Jessé had the inner joy that Jesus came to give us in the midst of every situation of life. This joy has nothing whatsoever to do with outward circumstances or other people. It comes only from within. You can't go to the store and buy it; no amount of money could ever pay for it. It is offered to us freely by our Lord and Savior.

Doña Jessé had learned that in the midst of turmoil and despair there was indeed a place of quiet rest near to the heart of God. She had grasped the profound truth that she could live through the darkness by what she had learned in the light. It was her deep love and knowledge of Jesus Christ gained in her year of study that lighted her way through the dark tunnel.

God never promised us a trouble-free life. Troubles and heartaches are the results of living in this sinful, fallen world. We will have crosses to bear from time to time, and some will be heavier than others. We may stumble and fall under the crushing weight, even as Jesus did long ago. But never forget this truth: Jesus never spoke of His cross without mentioning the glory that was to follow—His resurrection! Read through the Gospels and note that every time the cross is mentioned, the very next phrase speaks of the glorious resurrection. The cross and the glory are always intertwined, and the glory always follows the cross.

It was the glory I saw on Doña Jessé's face as she spoke of God's many blessings to her in the midst of such unbearable circumstances. I saw that luminous glow of the presence of God—that inner joy of the Lord. None of her outward circumstances had changed. Everyone was still just as sick; she still had all those people to feed three times a day; and she still had endless hours ahead of her with crying children. But she walked through her day, a moment at a time, in obedience to the Lord, and she discovered that the inner joy of the Lord was her strength. She was able to say, as Mary did after the resurrection, "I have seen the Lord!"

COMMITMENT

When we choose the obedient life, we are permitting God to make our lives all He dreamed they would become. We no longer need to ask what God's will is because we are continually living in His will. Our goal in life is obedience to Him in the midst of each situation.

Yesterday was Valentine's Day. And today as I thought about the valentine Harry gave me, many impressions came to mind. I found myself thanking God for the gift of love Harry and I have shared these past thirty-one years. I thought of all we have learned about each other in our life together. I recalled how our first friendship for one another grew into a lasting relationship of love. When we stood at the marriage altar, before God and the witnesses, we became one. We no longer walked down separate roads of life, but were on the same pathway, sharing our goals and interests. All that belonged to Harry became mine, and everything I had was now his. His wishes became my desires. I longed to know the needs of his life so I could somehow fill them. Things which were permissible before our marriage were no longer so because of the strong, yet gentle chord of love which bound us together. These unwritten laws have never proved burdensome or heavy. Rather, they have drawn us closer to one another. The result of our years together has been a deep-seated joy that touches every area of our lives.

Something like this happens in our obedient commitment to Jesus Christ, only to a far greater degree. We are united to Him in an eternal relationship of love. We no longer walk down the pathway of life alone because He is with us, guiding each step of the way. When we give ourself to Him in total commitment, many of the things we did before no longer seem desirable. We find His very wish becomes our command. All we have and ever hope to have belongs to Him. And all that He has belongs to us (Rom. 8:17). We yearn to know more about Him and look for ways to bring honor to His name. The strong, though gentle, chord of loving obedience binds us to Him, and it is never burdensome. The longer we serve Him, the dearer He grows to us. An inner joy springs from our union with Him, and it touches every area of our life.

The Christian lives in the delightful freedom of obedience and enjoys it! Our joy-filled life becomes a powerful demonstration of the reality of God in the world. The great plan and destiny God has ordained for us comes to fruition with obedience. God sees the limitless potential in our lives as we permit Him to work through us. He has the same trust and confidence in us that He had in His disciples long ago. He trusted that they would take His message of salvation to the dying world, and He has confidence that we will do the same. What an extraordinary concept this is—our faith and trust in Him and His faith and trust in us!

And on top of all this, the Bible tells us we become a sweet-smelling perfume, filling the world with the fragrance of God's love (2 Cor. 2:15). Our obedient life is a fragrant reflection of Him to those around us. Malcolm Muggeridge spoke of this beautiful fragrance when he wrote about Mother Teresa. As he left her at the train station in India, he said, "When the train began to move, and I walked away, I felt as though I were leaving behind me all the beauty and all the joy in the universe."[1]

God's call to us is still the same as it was to His disciples long ago, "Come and see." Come and see what it means to live the obedient life in Christ. Come and see the great potential that is waiting to be tapped by the Master. Come and see how your life can illuminate the dark corners of the suffering world around you as you take on the fragrant, luminous glow of the presence of God. Come and see that the bright stars of eternity are the obedient acts we do for God.

And in the end we make the ultimate discovery: Our greatest glory is in Jesus Christ, and His greatest glory is in us! This is the eternal joy of the obedient life.

Footnotes

Chapter 1

[1]Jim Wallis, "Conversion," *Sojourners Magazine* 7 (May 1978): 5.

[2]Use of poem by Bashō, from *An Introduction to Haiku: An Anthology of Poems and Poets from Bashō to Shiki,* by Harold G. Henderson. Copyright © 1958 by Harold G. Henderson. Used by permission of Doubleday and Company, Inc.

[3]Elisabeth Elliot, *The Liberty of Obedience* (Waco, Texas: Word Books, Publishers, 1976), p. 45. Used by permission of Word Books, Publishers, Waco, Texas, 76703.

Chapter 2

[1]Donald England, *A Christian View of Origins* (Grand Rapids, Mich.: Baker Book House).

Chapter 4

[1]Paris Reidhead, "Ten Shekels and a Shirt" (Minneapolis: Dimension Tapes, Bethany Fellowship, Inc.).

[2]Wallis, "Conversion," p. 6.

[3]Ibid.

Chapter 5

[1]John Piper, "Is Self-Love Biblical?" *Christianity Today* 22 (12 August 1977): 6. Used by permission.

Chapter 6

[1]Malcolm Muggeridge, *Something Beautiful for God* (New York: Harper and Row, 1971), Used by permission.

[2]Ibid.

[3]David E. Kucharsky, "At the Beginning," *Christianity Today* 22 (30 December 1977): 18. Used by permission.

Chapter 9

[1]Andrew Murray, *The School of Obedience* (Chicago: Moody Press), p. 37.

Chapter 10

[1]From *The Gospel of John, Vol. 2.,* p. 34. Translated and interpreted by William Barclay. Published in the U.S.A. by The Westminster Press, 1958. Used by permission.

[2]From *The Gospel of John, Vol. 1.,* p. 237. Translated and interpreted by William Barclay. Published in the U.S.A. by The Westminster Press, 1958. Used by permission.

Chapter 11

[1]Dorothy L. Sayers, *Creed or Chaos.* Copyright © 1949 by Dorothy L. Sayers. Copyright © renewed 1976 by Anthony Fleming. Used by permission of A. Watkins, Inc.

Chapter 12

[1]Muggeridge, *Something Beautiful.*